Blake Edwards: Interviews

Conversations with Filmmakers Series
Gerald Peary, General Editor

D1523244

Blake Edwards
INTERVIEWS

Edited by Gabriella Oldham

University Press of Mississippi / Jackson

www.upress.state.ms.us

The University Press of Mississippi is a member of the
Association of American University Presses.

First printing 2018

∞

Library of Congress Cataloging-in-Publication Data

Names: Edwards, Blake, 1922–2010, author. | Oldham, Gabriella, editor.
Title: Blake Edwards : interviews / edited by Gabriella Oldham.
Description: Jackson : University Press of Mississippi, 2018. | Series: Conversations with
filmmakers series | Includes index. |
Identifiers: LCCN 2017032090 (print) | LCCN 2017050126 (ebook) | ISBN 9781496815675
(epub single) | ISBN 9781496815682 (epub institutional) | ISBN 9781496815699 (pdf single) |
ISBN 9781496815705 (pdf institutional) | ISBN 9781496815668 (hardback)
Subjects: LCSH: Edwards, Blake, 1922–2010—Interviews. | Motion picture producers and
directors—United States—Interviews. | BISAC: PERFORMING ARTS / Individual Director
(see also BIOGRAPHY & AUTOBIOGRAPHY / Entertainment & Performing Arts). |
PERFORMING ARTS / Film & Video / Direction & Production. | BIOGRAPHY & AUTOBIOGRAPHY /
Entertainment & Performing Arts.
Classification: LCC PN1998.3.E33 (ebook) | LCC PN1998.3.E33 A5 2018 (print) | DDC
791.4302/33092—dc23
LC record available at https://lccn.loc.gov/2017032090

British Library Cataloging-in-Publication Data available

Contents

Introduction

I remember one critic saying, "We don't know who or what Blake Edwards is." Well, I didn't know either! I wanted to constantly explore, and if I found whatever it was I wanted most, then I would pursue that. But, you know, I'm *still* exploring; I don't think I have ever really found out "who or what Blake Edwards is." I just can't be labelled, and that is a helluva lot more stimulating for me.

In a 1977 interview with Peter Stamelman, Blake Edwards captured the essence of his identity with this statement. He was a multitalented and versatile artist constantly exploring who he was, not only in filmmaking but also in life. For most of his career he was typecast as a comedy director, but he also made films that probed heart-wrenching human drama. Edwards worked easily across many genres, producing a wide range of films that have contributed iconic images reflecting his culture and time. His strength as a filmmaker came from being a triple threat—writer, director, and producer—allowing him full control of his films, especially when the studio system failed him. Finally, his outspokenness and willingness to face and publicly share the darkest aspects of his life might have riled a few enemies in the business, but he also nurtured lifelong alliances with people who enacted his visions with artistry. Edwards had the capacity to revisit frustrations and failures in his work and demonstrate how critical it is to laugh at them in order to survive them. Reinventing himself many times throughout his sixty-year career, Edwards found new outlets of expression that fueled his creativity to the very end. This long-overdue collection of published articles presenting Blake Edwards in his own words explores the up and downs—and ups again—of a sometimes flawed but always gifted and often surprising filmmaker.

Edwards found it annoying to be labeled only as a comedy director, but he knew the genre intimately because it was so enmeshed in his everyday thinking. He was informally mentored—through osmosis, he would say—by studying the comic greats whose films he screened repeatedly: Buster Keaton, Preston Sturges, Frank Capra, and Laurel and Hardy. He was particularly influenced by Leo McCarey, with whom Edwards worked closely as a young writer and absorbed his stories of the "old days" of comedy making. Through these greats, Edwards developed a style that became known as sophisticated slapstick, in which the visual and physical—far more than the verbal—would trigger laughter, as it did in silent film. A layer of sophistication that Edwards added was humor that was not even seen but *implied* for the audience to imagine with only sound effects and music as clues to what happened. Hence, Cato ambushing Inspector Clouseau in the bath did not require a visual of that action, but merely the sight of Cato dashing into the offscreen bathroom, followed by water splashes and outraged exclamations, sufficiently secured the comedic effect in an intriguing way. Edwards often avoided "in-your-face" comedy even when relying on physicality and led his audiences above and beyond straight slapstick to react to the nonsense using their imagination.

From McCarey, Edwards adopted two principles of comedy that guided his understanding of what was innately funny and became trademarks of his work. In his interviews, Edwards frequently referred to the first principle, "topping the topper," as his discovery that one great gag could build to another unexpected gag which, when completed, could support yet *another* gag—thus, a logical chain of gags was tied to one scene, each surpassing the other and infusing unanticipated humor every step of the way. The scene then is exhausted for its comic potentials until it can go no further. So . . . a guy falls off a streetcar (gag 1); he recovers all his fallen possessions in a choreography of dodging and dancing through the traffic (gag 2); and then he rests after his efforts and becomes vulnerable to a startling twist of humor that follows seemingly out of nowhere (gag 3). Each new gag tops the topper of its predecessor. Edwards believed that any well-designed gag could succeed in its purpose on its own, but the wonderful build-up of comic tension fulfills and surpasses all expectations. The gags become logical punctuations to a situation that both imperils the hero and tests his stamina.

Edwards's second principle of comedy was what McCarey called "breaking the pain barrier," which resonated so strongly with Edwards that he not only applied it to his comedy, but used it as a mantra in his life. It is, in simple terms, reaching a breaking point with the absurdities and tragedies of life that all one can do is laugh. Edwards fondly retold McCarey's story of visiting a hospital as a board member and listening compassionately to an elderly woman as she narrated a series of catastrophic events that brought her and her husband to a dire conclusion. As the woman "topped the topper" with each woeful episode, McCarey felt a mounting tension from her narrative that climaxed with the final story of her husband being blown out of the hospital room and into the maternity ward when she lit a cigarette next to his oxygen tent. Despite his compassion for her, the chain of events was so extraordinary that McCarey erupted into uncontrollable laughter. For Edwards, this illuminating experience held a precious moral: one *must* laugh at life's absurdities to survive, or else the alternative is too dismal. Edwards's films incorporate this pain-barrier idea by intentionally featuring dark and violent situations that work as comic gags simply because of their absurdity. So . . . a despondent film executive tries to hang himself but the rope breaks—and he crashes through the floor right onto a vicious gossip columnist. He next inhales carbon monoxide in his car, but it rolls out of the garage, down a sand dune, and into the Pacific Ocean. As interviewer Kirk Honeycutt summarized Edwards's comic vision, there is "pain in every pratfall." Edwards never hesitated, especially in later years after decades of therapy, to say that he learned to recognize and accept this ironic reality in his own life. To illustrate this irony, he described to Larry King in vivid detail how one day, when determined to commit suicide on a beach, Edwards was interrupted by his dog, whom he distracted by throwing a ball which caused him to dislocate his shoulder. As he fell over, he stepped on a razor blade he had discarded, and called Emergency for fear he would bleed to death. That Edwards could ultimately laugh at this funny story, as he called it, was a reality check that he could survive anything life threw at him. At the heart of Edwards's comedy, then, is a slapstick world inhabited by real-life people who persist in making (or trying to make) sense of nonsense. This honest view of life is, of necessity, always perched on the threshold between comedy and tragedy, where one can sit laughing until it hurts and hurting until one laughs. Both extremes simultaneously make one, in Edwards's final estimation, fully alive.

Continually testing his abilities as a writer, which he considered himself to be above all other professions, Edwards did not hesitate to strip straight comedy from his films in ventures that purposefully explored other genres with sharp insight. Such detours focused on creating thrilling suspense (*Experiment in Terror*), rugged westerns (*Wild Rovers*), riveting drama (*Days of Wine and Roses*), and bittersweet romance (*Breakfast at Tiffany's*). These have been considered some of Edwards's finest films in his decades-long career. He of course also created musicals, namely *Darling Lili* and *Victor/Victoria*, showcasing the talents of his wife Julie Andrews. Edwards's deft handling of different genres was nurtured in his early work in radio and television, especially in creating a series of successful private eyes and gamblers (Richard Diamond, Peter Gunn, Mr. Lucky). He thought that emotions could be heightened particularly when they were juxtaposed to the everyday world. Thus, his characters in these genre films have complex yet familiar lives, challenges, and dynamics, whether as family members or love interests. They ebb and flow between states of despair and hope while struggling with codependency, loss, regret, confusion, and self-denial. In these films' endings, Edwards often leaned toward ambiguity and uncertainty about the outcome because he likely believed that life offered no easy solution or resolution, only the chance to hope for one. It is telling that Edwards often said he would have preferred to make *Breakfast at Tiffany's* truer to Truman Capote's novella, with its darker overtones of sexual ambiguity and materialism, but he knew that neither the studio nor Audrey Hepburn would have accepted that ending. As a result, the film has become, in the words of Capote's biographer Gerald Clarke, a "sugar and spice confection," but nonetheless it remains an iconic film of its time, thanks to endearing performances, fashion influences, and a poignant hit song. Nevertheless, Edwards recognized what he considered a compromised ending and aspired in his own productions to create honest portraits of characters who were caught between their dreams and reality. One can only imagine the potential power of some of Edwards's unrealized dramatic projects as he grew more philosophical about life: *Gettysburg* was intended to be a story of the bloody battle as seen through the eyes of the townspeople living in its midst; *The Toy Soldier* would have brought back Jack Lemmon as a father coping with grief over his young dying son. Edwards even entertained the idea of directing *Planet of the Apes* which, through his unique lens, would certainly have had a most curious interpretation.

Given his versatility in what Steven Gaydos called "going hyphenate" as writer-director-producer and crossing film genres with relative ease, Edwards developed a healthy intolerance for any questioning of his artistic creativity and professional expertise. It was healthy in that Edwards knew he could follow his instincts when he alone held the reins of filmmaking, not only writing and directing but also producing with a familial team he entrusted to execute his vision. Perhaps Edwards's most productive partnership was with composer Henry Mancini on thirty films over thirty-five years. Starting with the score for the television series *Peter Gunn* and the catchy Pink Panther theme, Mancini's talent for creating unforgettable melodies gave Edwards's films some of its venerable awards with the hits "Days of Wine and Roses" and "Moon River," which the American Film Institute selected in 2004 as the fourth most memorable song in film history. Edwards also worked consistently with editor Ralph E. Winters, producer Tony Adams, and regular cinematographers over numerous films. He even involved his doctors as co-writers or actors in his films. As well, he employed his children from his first marriage to Patricia Walker—daughter Jennifer, who acted in a number of films, and son Geoffrey, who shared writing credits. Among his actors, Edwards made lifelong friends who would resurface in multiple films, and, because he knew what it felt like to be an actor in his early show business career under not always pleasant circumstances, he helped his stars bring out their best. Jack Lemmon, whom Edwards often called his favorite actor, said that had it not been for the depthful performance Edwards elicited from him in *Days of Wine and Roses*, he would never have won his Oscar for *Save the Tiger*. Dudley Moore, whom Edwards knew from their group therapy sessions, stepped into *10* when George Segal dropped out, and was so ecstatic to be in a film which rejuvenated his career that he even agreed to appear "bottomless" for a scene—a joking reference Moore later made to the scene in which Julie Andrews appeared topless in *S.O.B.* Andrews would, of course, become Edwards's leading lady, both professionally and personally, and his staunchest supporter in times of great rage and depression with the industry. Despite being "Blackie," a nickname those closest to him used because of his volatile moods, Edwards was known to create a comfortable set, although one actor would prove to be at continual odds with his director. Peter Sellers, whom Edwards acknowledged as a comic genius and an actor of incredible range, was relentlessly self-absorbed and self-destructive, often lost in his own mind and erratic behavior. Edwards frequently cited his exasperation with Sellers, including the time the actor called him in the middle of the night to announce he had just spoken with God about a scene on the latest Pink Panther movie. The next day, Edwards allowed Sellers to act according to divine direction, but upon seeing the disastrous result, advised him, "The next time you talk to God, tell him to stay out of show business!" The sarcasm did not fare well with Sellers, and their relationship in five Panther films deteriorated to a money-making relationship and tension-filled collaboration. However, given the ongoing success of the series and lucrative worldwide merchandising (from Pink Panther corn flakes to bubble bath), Edwards had earned the freedom to create his own schedule and pursue his own ideas, especially when the industry betrayed his trust in it.

Edwards's answer to professional assaults on his integrity as a filmmaker would manifest in an inevitable comedy film, but in such circumstances the comedies were not renditions of his sophisticated slapstick. Instead, they were vitriolic autobiographical diatribes that skewered Hollywood and all its worst elements. It is easy to regard Edwards's satiric films as a barometer of his outrage, his deep-rooted anguish, and—eventually—his personal recovery. Studio executives considered Edwards a director who was extravagant with *their* budgets, an accusation he always denied vehemently because he had worked with Columbia's tight-fisted Harry Cohn, who taught him all about the budget game. However, Edwards upheld his belief that he would do whatever was best for the film, in spite of the budget, because a good film would attract big box office, which would more than offset the cost. Notwithstanding, the debacle that *Darling Lili* proved to be in 1970 was one of the sorest touchstones in Edwards's career and in Hollywood history; it is often equated with Cimino's *Heaven's Gate* fiasco ten years later. Edwards recounted his bitter experience in which the studio insisted on shooting *Darling Lili* in Ireland, despite his warnings about the bleak weather and suggestions for thriftier solutions. The overall result was an unprecedented financial loss for the studio and mud-slinging that placed the onus squarely on Edwards for treating the film as an extravagant love letter to Julie Andrews.

This unfortunate experience was followed by two more insults-to-injury. First, without Edwards's knowledge, MGM editorially butchered his three-hour *Wild Rovers* (1971), which he had conceived as a Greek tragedy set in the American West.

Edwards later blamed studio head James Aubrey for cutting out the heart of the story, even changing the ending to an inappropriate upbeat version. Edwards subsequently disowned the film that had been his labor of love, while those few who had seen the original director's cut considered it one of his best. To appease Edwards's outrage, Aubrey then offered him control over *The Carey Treatment* (1972) but reneged and again decimated Edwards's vision in the editing room. Humiliated and depressed over this utter disrespect, Edwards later admitted he obsessed about killing Aubrey. He was only jolted from this fixation when he nearly hit a jogger whom, he discovered to his shock as he looked in the rearview mirror, just happened to be Aubrey. Edwards suddenly realized how his loathing of the studio system was even controlling his subconscious. Although he filed a breach of contract suit against MGM, the professional and psychic damage had been done: the studios considered the director anathema, and Edwards's emotional and mental state needed healing. He fled Hollywood for Switzerland, vowing never to return.

During this retreat, Edwards suffered greatly from his own "demons," as he often called his dark states of mind, for long periods unable to work while Andrews continued her career with mixed results. In short, both Edwards and Andrews had become Hollywood scapegoats, blamed for the mismanagement and ignorance of the corporate bigwigs at Paramount and MGM over what quality filmmaking required. As Edwards told Myron Meisel in his 1981 interview about that dark time, "For all that the style of the studio executive has changed, the need for a scapegoat in reserve is more important to them than either the commercial or artistic wisdom of a particular course." When Edwards finally roused his energy into creative work again, which he sorely missed, he returned to producing, writing, and directing multiple sequels of the surefire Panther series to his own standards. But brewing in his mind was his last word on the subject in the form he knew best to retaliate against these injustices: he would write a comedy. Edwards produced two widely acclaimed autobiographical comedies that enacted his personal fantasies on the screen at this time, drawing on his skills as producer, writer, and director. The first film, *10*, helped him exorcise his demons about aging and reinstated his reputation as a top director. It opened as number one in the United States and as one of the top-grossing films of 1979. Reviewer Gene Siskel of the *Chicago Tribune* called it "a gentle essay on the problems of male menopause." The second film, *S.O.B.* (the acronym for Standard Operating Business, although the other, more mundane interpretation lies prominently beneath the surface), was Edwards's poison pen letter to Hollywood. As Vincent Canby wrote in the *New York Times*, "It's a nasty, biased, self-serving movie that also happens to be hilarious most of the time. . . . Mr. Edwards . . . is here pouring out his heart—which pumps pure bile—about his own ups and downs with the Hollywood establishment of the early '70s." His acid depiction of life in Hollywood also fired a shocking barb, with his wife's consent, at her Hollywoodized sweet-saccharine persona in *Mary Poppins* and *The Sound of Music*. Andrews plays a producer's wife who uses foul language and agrees to "show my boobies" in order to save her film-husband's flailing picture. Both films not only served their purpose—to outrage Hollywood and attack the enemy—but also helped Edwards recover from his devastating blows by creating entertainment with a message. Hollywood powers recognized themselves in *S.O.B.*, but Edwards gleefully knew if they sued, they would only be identifying their culpability. When Hollywood agent Sue Mengers suspected that the bitchy Shelley Winters character in *S.O.B.* was modeled after her, she announced, "An Alp should only fall on their house." Edwards simply answered that an Alp was preferable to Mengers doing so.

In his later films, Edwards continued exploring his own issues through his screenplays. Much could be said about his films relating to male-female relationships and, specifically, role reversals in a film aptly named *Switch* and the award-winning *Victor/Victoria* (which led Edwards into directing for theater). In a 1991 interview with Daniel Schweiger, Edwards mentioned that since he obviously knew what men were about, he was more interested in understanding women who "have been an enormous puzzlement. They've created a lot of ambivalence in my life, with pleasure and angst." Edwards himself was long a subject of gossip about his own sexual orientation; at one point he was even thought to have AIDS because of an illness which later was diagnosed as the Epstein-Barr virus. To these accusations Edwards usually retorted as he did in a 1990 *Positif* interview, "It is so typical of this city. There has been this rumor that I have been a homosexual since I started in this business, and nothing is further from the truth. I don't say this to boast. In fact, to those that traffic in this, I say, 'Listen, if you want to discuss it, I can only tell you that if I were gay I would be the first to admit it.'" But Edwards often spoke of his fascination with exploring homosexuality in his films. More so, though, it was simply the issue of sexuality that intrigued him, and he created enough ambiguity about sexual roles (carried to the nth degree by Andrews in *Victor/Victoria*, who played a woman playing a male impersonator pretending to be a female impersonator) that for Edwards, it was always reduced to one bottom line. As he responded to Raffaele Caputo's question on the layers of his subtle humor, "What I set out to do is exorcise my own demons, to make myself laugh at things which, to one degree or another, represent other people . . . sometimes it works and sometimes it doesn't."

Edwards's "therapeutic" films were brave efforts to reach the core of his own issues, even though in fact they sometimes worked and sometimes did not for critics and audiences. One such film was Edwards's most intimate family-affair self-revelation in *That's Life!* Edwards not only shot the film in his Malibu home, but cast Andrews, daughter Jennifer, Jack Lemmon, and Lemmon's son Chris and wife Felicia Farr. The plot, centering on one weekend in the life of this family, seemed, in the final analysis, to be very much like analysis. Edwards depicted himself as a self-centered man having nightmares about aging and death, neglecting his family's needs until his long-suffering wife helps him reach an important realization. Edwards's daughter later revealed to *People* magazine how close to home the film was, given her father's harsh rejection of her many years before at a critical point in her life. Another subplot involved Andrews's character undergoing a biopsy on her throat to determine if she would be able to sing again (the film has a happy outcome, while the reality for Andrews eventually proved tragic). Acknowledging the risk Edwards took in being so disquietingly forthright, *Los Angeles Times* reviewer Michael Wilmington thought its topics of "familial strife, decay, and mortality . . . far from gloomy: This is one of the funniest, and perhaps the most life-embracing, movies Edwards has made in the '80s. The currents of despair give the humor a deeper bite." Wilmington also captured the impact of such a film that "took considerable courage, love, and craft to make. Watching it—accepting, enjoying, and even, occasionally, forgiving it—is like having a real conversation with a human being, a rare enough gift for any current film to offer."

Edwards's work, and his evolution as a filmmaker as well as a deeply reflective human being, continually placed faith in how he translated life—his life, all lives—into cinematic terms. Some critics and audiences may have cringed at the intensely personal revelations—all the more difficult to watch when the fictional element was removed and direct parallels to real people were identified. But there was also value in seeing that one could let the world witness and even judge such personal stories, while those involved in the chaos would not only remain friends but also grow with each other because of their communal suffering, grounded with humor. When seen in this light, Edwards's films represent, unintentionally or otherwise, wise advice for many lost souls.

James Ulmer reporting for *Hollywood Reporter* on Edwards's tribute at the Cannes Film Festival in 1992 stated that Edwards clearly knew his pariah status. "I've been such a severe critic of the establishment for so many years it's second nature," Edwards noted. "I don't want to be mixed up with them, and they don't want to be mixed up with me." Still, Edwards seemed to find pride and strength in being a thorn in Hollywood's side because of his personal versatility and an outlook that inevitably pulled him back from the dark side. As he mentioned to interviewers Lehman and Luhr, he was "an emotional juggler. I always have five or six things that are unclear, but precise enough to juggle. At some point I throw them in the air, and, depending on what falls first or what I see first, I rush ahead because I could play this game forever of choosing what I'll use." Variety for Edwards was not just a recipe for staying fresh and interested; it was a survival mechanism. In his last years, Edwards expanded his repertoire with an intense indulgence in painting and sculpting as new forms of therapy; he particularly found the angles in sculpting well connected to directing. Edwards also admitted to having a "Clouseau gene," which made him, like his bumbling detective alter ego, especially vulnerable to life's serendipitous and sometimes cruel accidents. However, he seemed to have come full circle in understanding and accepting who he was by the end of his life. He had continually walked a fine line between comedy and drama, not necessarily wanting to, but certainly finding ways to remain standing upright in the process. His pratfalls were only the steps he had to endure to live by what he often touted as his 11th Commandment: "Thou shalt not give up." For Edwards, never giving up ensured that his voice would be heard when he was ready to speak, accompanied always by both a sigh and a laugh.

Acknowledgments

Seeking permissions for a book like this often makes me feel like Inspector Jacques Clouseau, bumbling after one clue and another. Fortunately, thanks to the gracious assistance of many individuals, I did not bumble as much as I might have on my own.

I would like to acknowledge all who researched and granted permissions for the articles included in this book: Bobby Dicks (CNN Collection); Jovita Dominguez (Directors Guild of America); Ralph Drew (*Los Angeles Times*); Aryn Glazier (Dolph Briscoe Center for American History in Austin, Texas); Michael E. Fogel (Hearst Newspapers); Shari Goldsmith (Hearst Newspapers); Lisa S. Lima (Eastman Kodak Company); Kari Mozena (*Los Angeles* magazine); Rosie Norwood-Kelly (Condé Nast); Jesse Peers (George Eastman Museum); Mike Pepin (American Film Institute—special thanks for his time in double-checking the transcript); William Van Niekerken (*San Francisco Chronicle*); and Erica Varela (*Los Angeles Times*).

I was deeply touched by the generosity of the authors/interviewers who granted permission to reprint their work. When I described the book to them, they all showed delight and support for this tribute to a man they loved and admired. I am pleased to share this book with each of them because their articles have contributed so much to giving us a fuller portrait of Blake Edwards in his own words: Julia Cameron, Susan Cameron, Raffaele Caputo, Bill Desowitz, Kirk Honeycutt, Jed Horne, Rena Dictor Le Blanc, Darrah Meeley, Myron Meisel, Jerry Roberts, Daniel Schweiger, and Peter Stamelman. I also want to thank Steven Gaydos and James Ulmer for their kind words of support.

I very much appreciate the meticulous assistance of Kristine Krueger at the National Film Information Service, Margaret Herrick Library, Academy of Motion Picture Arts and Sciences in arranging for me to view the microfiche on Blake Edwards in New York.

Thanks to Paul Damian Rossi for his excellent translation of the *Positif* interview.

It was a pleasure to meet Michele Mattei during her trip to New York to discuss the use of her sensitive portrait of Blake Edwards for the cover. I not only appreciated her gracious permission to do so, but am grateful for the chance to learn more about her extraordinary photography.

Thanks to Emily Bandy and all at University Press of Mississippi for handling the meticulous aspects of this book's production. Special gratitude to director Craig Gill for his ever-positive emails, sage advice, and supportive attention to this book.

GO

Chronology

1922   Born William Blake Crump in Tulsa, Oklahoma, on July 26, son of Donald and Lillian (Grommett) Crump. His father left before he was born, and Lillian remarried Jack McEdward (stepfather). Grandfather was J. Gordon Edwards, a director of silent film (Blake eventually adopted Edwards as his name).

1925   Family moves to Los Angeles, where Jack becomes a film production manager.

1940s   After high school, Blake works as an actor with John Ford, William Wyler, and Otto Preminger; acting roles (often uncredited) include a cadet in *Ten Gentlemen from West Point* (1942), an airman in *Thirty Seconds Over Tokyo* (1944), a lieutenant in *In the Meantime, Darling* (1944), and a soldier in *The Best Years of Our Lives* (1946). Proves to be too rebellious to take direction. Serves in the US Coast Guard but suffers a catastrophic back injury when he jokingly dives into a shallow Beverly Hills swimming pool, fracturing his skull and breaking his neck. Lays in traction for five months.

1948   Produces and writes screenplay *Panhandle* (with John Champion).

1949   Produces and writes screenplay *Stampede* (with John Champion).

1949–53 Creates, writes, and directs radio program *Richard Diamond, Private Detective*.

1950   Writes episode #14 for radio show *Broadway Is My Beat*.

1950–52 Writes multiple episodes for radio show *The Lineup*.

1951   Writes multiple episodes for radio show *Suspense*.

1951–53 Writes multiple episodes for radio show *Yours Truly, Johnny Dollar*.

1952   Writes *Sound Off* and *Castle in the Air* with Richard Quine. Writes one episode ("The Long Night") for *Invitation Playhouse: Mind Over Murder* (TV series).

1952–54 Writes multiple episodes and directs five episodes for *Four Star Playhouse* (TV series).

1953   Writes *All Ashore*, directed by Richard Quine, in which Patricia Walker has a role; Edwards marries Walker.

1954   Writes story with Benedict Freedman and John Fenton Murray for *The Atomic Kid*, starring Mickey Rooney. Writes "Cop Killer" for *The Lineup* (TV series). Writes screenplay for *Drive a Crooked Road*, directed by Richard Quine. Writes and directs TV movie *Mickey Spillane's "Mike Hammer!"* Directs "Death, the Hard Way" for *The Pepsi-Cola Playhouse* (TV series). Directs "Midnight Supper" for *City Detective* (TV series).

1954–55   Creates and writes with Richard Quine multiple episodes for *The Mickey Rooney Show: Hey, Mulligan* (TV series). Writes scripts for *Richard Diamond, Private Detective* for NBC.

1955   Writes with Richard Quine and directs *Bring Your Smile Along*. Writes screenplay for *My Sister Eileen*, directed by Richard Quine. Writes "The Smuggler" and directs "Big Joe's Comin' Home" for *Jane Wyman Presents the Fireside Theatre* (TV series). Directs "Safe Journey" for *The Star and the Story* (TV series).

1956   Writes with Richard Quine and directs *He Laughed Last*. Writes "Double Cross" for *Chevron Hall of Stars* (TV series). Writes "The Payoff" for *The Ford Television Theatre* (TV series).

1957   Writes with Leo Rosten and directs *Mister Cory*. Writes with Arthur Carter and Jed Harris screenplay for *Operation Mad Ball*. Writes "The Tycoon" for *The Adventures of McGraw* (TV series). Writes "The Smuggler" for *Studio 57* (TV series). Daughter Jennifer Edwards (née Jennifer B. McEdward) born.

1957–60   Creates characters for *Richard Diamond, Private Detective* (TV series, 77 episodes total).

1959–60   Creates and writes some episodes for *Mr. Lucky* (34 episodes total).

1958   Writes and directs screenplay for *This Happy Feeling*. Directs *The Perfect Furlough*. Nominated with Arthur Carter and Jed Harris for Writers Guild of America Award (Screen) for Best Written American Comedy for *Operation Mad Ball*.

1958–61   Creates and writes various episodes for *Peter Gunn* (TV series, 110 episodes total).

1959   Creates, writes, and directs *Peter Gunn* with Craig Stevens and music by Henry Mancini. Produces *Mr. Lucky* with John Vivyan and Ross Martin for CBS, with music by Henry Mancini. Directs first big-budget movie, *Operation Petticoat*, for Universal. Son Geoffrey Edwards (née Geoffrey B. McEdward) born. Nominated for Primetime Emmy Awards: Best Direction of a Single Program of a Dramatic Series— Less Than One Hour and Best Writing of a Single Program of a Dramatic Series—Less Than One Hour ("The Kill," *Peter Gunn*).

1960   Directs *High Time*. Nominated for Edgar Allan Poe Award for Best Episode in a TV Series ("The Comic," *Peter Gunn*).

1961   Directs *Breakfast at Tiffany's*. Creates and writes some episodes for *Dante* (TV series).

1962   Directs *Days of Wine and Roses*. Produces and directs *Experiment in Terror*. Nominated for Directors Guild Award for Outstanding Directorial Achievement in Motion Pictures for *Breakfast at Tiffany's*. Nominated for Golden Laurel Award as Top Director (8th Place). Writes with Larry Gelbert screenplay for *The Notorious Landlady*, directed by Richard Quine. Writes episodes for *The Dick Powell Theatre* (TV series). Writes story for *The Couch*.

1963   Creates, writes, and directs *The Pink Panther*. Nominated for Golden Globe, Best Director, *Days of Wine and Roses*. Wins OCIC Award at San Sebastián International Film Festival for *Days of Wine and Roses* (ties with *A Night to Remember*). Nominated with Larry Gelbert for Writers Guild of America Award (Screen) for Best Written American Comedy for *The Notorious Landlady*.

1964   Writes with William Peter Blatty *A Shot in the Dark*. Nominated for Golden Laurel Award as Top Director (5th Place).

1965   Directs *The Great Race*. Wins 2nd Place Golden Laurel Award as Director. Nominated for Grand Prix for *The Great Race* at the Moscow International Film Festival. Nominated with Maurice Richlin for Writers Guild of America Award for Best Written American Comedy for *The Pink Panther*.

1966   Produces and directs *What Did You Do in the War, Daddy?* Nominated for Golden Laurel Award as Producer-Director (4th Place).

1967   Produces, writes with William Peter Blatty, and directs *Gunn*. Divorces Patricia. Nominated for Golden Laurel Award as Producer-Director (4th Place).

1968   Produces, writes, and directs *The Party* with Peter Sellers. Creates concept/character for *Inspector Clouseau*.Wins 3rd Place Golden Laurel Award as Producer-Director.

1969   Creates concepts for *The Pink Panther Show* (TV series, 12 episodes). Marries Julie Andrews, whose daughter Emma Walton joins the family, and adopts two orphans from Vietnam, Amelia Leigh and Joanna Lynne in the 1970s.

1970   Produces, writes with William Peter Blatty, and directs *Darling Lili*, a financial disaster, costing $17 million and bringing Paramount Pictures to near-financial collapse.

1971   Produces, writes, and directs *Wild Rovers*. MGM removes Edwards from film and drastically cuts the film. Edwards disowns it.

1972   Directs *The Carey Treatment*, with the understanding that he would have final say after the *Wild Rovers* butchering, only to have MGM radically re-edit the film. Abandons Hollywood for Switzerland.

1974   Writes and directs *The Tamarind Seed* with Julie Andrews.

1975   Produces, writes, and directs *The Return of the Pink Panther*, the third in the series.

1976   Produces, writes, and directs *The Pink Panther Strikes Again*.

1977   Wins Evening Standard British Film Award for Best Comedy, *The Return of the Pink Panther*. Wins with Frank Waldman Writers Guild of America Award (Screen) for Best Comedy Adapted from Another Medium for *The Pink Panther Strikes Again*.

1978   Produces, writes, and directs *Revenge of the Pink Panther*. Wins Evening Standard British Film Award for Best Comedy, *The Pink Panther Strikes Again*.

1979   Produces, writes, and directs *10*. Wins Evening Standard British Film Award for Best Comedy, *Revenge of the Pink Panther*.

1980   Peter Sellers dies, and Edwards uses archival footage from previous Panther films to include Sellers in *Trail of the Pink Panther*. Nominated for National Society of Film Critics Award as Best Director (4th Place) and Best Screenplay (5th Place) for *10*. Nominated for Writers Guild of America Award (Screen) for Best Comedy Written Directly for the Screen for *10*.

1981   Produces, writes, and directs *S.O.B.*, an autobiographical satire that skewers Hollywood based on his devastating experiences with *Darling Lili*, *Wild Rovers*, and *The Carey Treatment*. Shatters image of Julie Andrews's sweet *Mary Poppins/Sound of Music* character when she goes topless.

1982   Produces, writes, and directs *Victor/Victoria*. Produces, writes, and directs *Trail of the Pink Panther*. Nominated for Razzie Award as Worst Director and Worst Screenplay for *S.O.B.* Nominated for Writers Guild of America Award (Screen) for Best Comedy Written Directly for the Screen for *S.O.B.*

1983   Produces, writes with son Geoffrey, and directs *Curse of the Pink Panther*. Produces and writes with Milton Wexler and son Geoffrey *The Man Who Loved Women*. Nominated for an Academy Award for *Victor/Victoria* (Best Writing, Screenplay Based on Material from Another Medium). Wins César Award (France) for Best Foreign Film, David di Donatello Award for Best Foreign Screenplay, and Sant Jordi

Award for Best Foreign Film for *Victor/Victoria*. Wins Writers Guild of America (Screen) Award for Best Comedy Adapted from Another Medium for *Victor/Victoria*.

1984   Directs *Micki and Maude*. Writes story for *City Heat* (as Sam O. Brown). Writes *The Ferret* (unrealized).

1986   Writes and directs *A Fine Mess* and *That's Life*; Mancini/Bricusse song "Life in a Looking Glass" nominated for both an Academy Award and Golden Globe (Best Original Song) as well as a Golden Raspberry Award (Worst Original Song); Golden Globe nominations for Julie Andrews and Jack Lemmon for Best Performances in a Comedy/ Musical.

1987   Directs *Blind Date*.

1988   Writes and directs *Sunset*. Wins Creative Achievement Award from the American Comedy Awards, USA.

1989   Writes and directs *Skin Deep*. Writes TV movie *Peter Gunn*. Writes "Justin Case" for *Walt Disney's Wonderful World of Color* (TV series). Wins Razzie Award as Worst Director of *Sunset*. Displays two bronze sculptures at Century Plaza Towers, part of the Third Sculpture Walk produced by the Los Angeles Arts Council.

1990   Wins Career Achievement Award from the Los Angeles Film Critics Association.

1991   Writes and directs *Switch*. Receives Star on the Walk of Fame in Hollywood (April 3 at 6908 Hollywood Boulevard).

1991–92   Invited to recut and remix *Darling Lili* by Michael Schlesinger, Head of Paramount's Repertory division; director's cut is twenty-nine minutes shorter than the original. Fully restored, Dolby SR 35mm print premiers at 1992 Cannes Film Festival during retrospective of Edwards's films; US premiere is at Directors Guild Theatre in Los Angeles.

1993   Writes and directs *Son of the Pink Panther*. Concepts are used for *The Pink Panther* (TV series) and *Pink Goes to Hollywood* (video game). Wins Preston Sturges Award from the Directors Guild of America, USA.

1995   Writes TV movie *Victor/Victoria*.

1995–99   Writes, produces, and directs *Victor/Victoria* on Broadway; music by Henry Mancini and Frank Wildhorn (after Mancini's death); lyrics by Leslie Bricusse and Frank Wildhorn. Productions: 1995, Minneapolis, Chicago, Broadway (New York); 1998, National Tour; 2003, Stockholm; 2005, Madrid; 2010, Vienna; 2012, London. Julie Andrews is nominated for the only Tony Award for the show, but she rejects the nomination because she feels the cast and crew have been "egregiously overlooked." Drama Desk Award nomination for Outstanding Actress in a Musical (Andrews), Outstanding Featured Actress in a Musical (Rachel York), and Outstanding Set Design.

1997   Produces off-Broadway production of *Minor Demons*.

1998   Wins Distinguished Achievement Award from Hamptons International Film Festival.

1999   Writes, produces, and directs off-Broadway production of *Big Rosemary*, adapted from 1956 film *He Laughed Last*.

2000   Wins Contribution to Cinematic Imagery Award from Art Directors Guild.

2001   Wins Lifetime Achievement Award at Rhode Island International Film Festival.

2002   Wins Laurel Award for Screen Writing Achievement, Writers Guild of America, USA.

2004   Receives Honorary Academy Award from the Academy of Motion Pictures Arts and Science "in recognition of his writing, directing, and producing an extraordinary body of work for the screen." Wins Life Career Award from the Academy of Science Fiction, Fantasy, and Horror Films, USA.

2006   Writes *The Pink Panther*.

2009   Writes *The Pink Panther 2*. Retrospective of 130 paintings and sculptures in "The Art of Blake Edwards" at the Pacific Design Center. Receives French Legion of Honor for outstanding contributions to the arts.

2010   Writes two episodes for *Pink Panther and Pals* (TV series). Nominated for Gold Derby Awards for Life Achievement (Performer). Dies December 15 of complications of pneumonia in Santa Monica, California.

2013   Posthumously inducted into Online Film and Television Association Film Hall of Fame.

Filmography

These are credits as film director. Edwards has numerous credits as writer and producer only in television, film, radio, and theater. See Chronology for additional credits.

BRING YOUR SMILE ALONG (1955)
Columbia Pictures
Producer: Jonie Taps
Director: **Blake Edwards**
Screenplay: **Blake Edwards**, Richard Quine
Cinematography: Charles Lawton Jr.
Editing: Al Clark
Music: Paul Mason Howard
Cast: Frankie Laine (Jerry Dennis), Keefe Brasselle (Martin "Marty" Adams), Constance Towers (Nancy Willows), Lucy Marlow (Marge Stevenson), William Leslie (David Parker), Mario Siletti (Ricardo), Ruth Warren (Mrs. Klein, Landlady), Jack Albertson (Mr. Jenson), Bobby Clark (Waldo), Murray Leonard (Dave), Ida Smeraldo (Mama)
Color, 83 minutes

HE LAUGHED LAST (1956)
Columbia Pictures
Producer: Jonie Taps
Director: **Blake Edwards**
Screenplay: **Blake Edwards**, Richard Quine
Cinematography: Henry Freulich
Editing: Jack Ogilvie
Music: Arthur Morton
Cast: Frankie Laine (Gino Lupo), Lucy Marlow (Rosemary "Rosie" Lebeau), Anthony Dexter (Dominic Rodriguez), Richard Long (Jimmy Murphy), Alan Reed (Big Dan Hennessy), Jesse White (Max Lassiter), Florenz Ames (George Eagle), Henry Slate (Ziggy)
Color, 77 minutes

MISTER CORY (1957)
Universal-International
Producer: Robert Arthur
Director: **Blake Edwards**
Screenplay: **Blake Edwards**, Leo Rosten
Cinematography: Russell Metty
Music: Henry Mancini
Cast: Tony Curtis (Cory), Martha Hyer (Abby), Charles Bickford (Caldwell/Biloxi),
    Kathryn Grant (Jen)
Color, 92 minutes

THIS HAPPY FEELING (1958)
Universal-International
Producer: Ross Hunter
Director: **Blake Edwards**
Screenplay: **Blake Edwards**, F. Hugh Herbert
Cinematography: Arthur E. Arling
Music: Frank Skinner
Cast: Debbie Reynolds (Janet Blake), Curd Jürgens (Preston Mitchell), John Saxon
    (Bill Tremaine), Alexis Smith (Nita Hollaway), Mary Astor (Miss Tremaine),
    Estelle Winwood (Miss Early), Troy Donahue (Tony Manza), Hayden Rorke
    (Mister Booth), Gloria Holden (Miss Dover), Alex Gerry (Mister Dover), Joe
    Flynn (Doctor McCafferty)
Color, 92 minutes

THE PERFECT FURLOUGH (1958)
Universal-International
Producer: Robert Arthur
Director: **Blake Edwards**
Screenplay: Stanley Shapiro
Cinematography: Philip Lathrop
Music: Dámaso Pérez Prado
Cast: Tony Curtis (Cpl. Paul Hodges), Janet Leigh (Lt. Vicki Loren), Keenan Wynn
    (Harvey Franklin), Linda Cristal (Sandra Roca, the Argentine Bombshell),
    Elaine Stritch (Liz Baker), Marcel Dalio (Henri Valentin), Les Tremayne (Col.
    Leland), Jay Novello (Rene Valentin), King Donovan (Maj. Collins), Gordon
    Jones ("Sylvia," MP #1), Alvy Moore (Pvt. Marvin Brewer), Lilyan Chauvin
    (French nurse), Troy Donahue (Sgt. Nickles), Dick Crockettas (Hans, MP #2),
    Eugene Borden (French doctor)
Color, 93 minutes

OPERATION PETTICOAT (1959)
Universal-International
Producer: Robert Arthur
Director: **Blake Edwards**
Screenplay: Paul King, Joseph B. Stone, Stanley J. Shapiro, Maurice Richlin
Cinematography: Russell Harlan
Editing: Frank Gross, Ted J. Kent
Music: David Rose, Henry Mancini (uncredited)
Cast: Cary Grant (Lieutenant Commander Matthew T. "Matt" Sherman), Tony
    Curtis (Lieutenant, Junior Grade Nicholas "Nick" Holden), Joan O'Brien (Sec-
    ond Lieutenant Dolores Crandall), Dina Merrill (Second Lieutenant Barbara
    Duran), Gene Evans (Chief Torpedoman "Mo" Molumphry), Dick (Richard)
    Sargent (Ensign Stovall), Arthur O'Connell (Chief Motor Machinist's Mate
    Sam Tostin), Virginia Gregg (Major Edna Heywood), Robert F. Simon (Cap-
    tain J. B. Henderson), Robert Gist (Lieutenant Watson), Gavin MacLeod (Yeo-
    man Ernest Hunkle), George Dunn (Prophet of Doom), Dick Crockett (Petty
    Officer Harmon), Madlyn Rhue (Second Lieutenant Reid), Marion Ross (Sec-
    ond Lieutenant Colfax), Clarence Lung (Sergeant Ramon Gallardo), Frankie
    Darro (Pharmacist's Mate 3rd Class Dooley), Tony Pastor Jr. (Fox)
Color, 124 minutes

HIGH TIME (1960)
20th Century Fox
Producer: Charles Brackett
Director: **Blake Edwards**
Screenplay: Frank Waldman, Tom Waldman
Cinematography: Ellsworth Fredericks
Editing: Robert L. Simpson
Music: Henry Mancini
Cast: Bing Crosby (Harvey Howard), Fabian (Gil Sparrow), Tuesday Weld (Joy El-
    der), Nicole Maurey (Prof. Helene Gauthier), Richard Beymer (Bob Banner-
    man), Patrick Adiarte (T. J. Padmanagham), Yvonne Craig (Randy "Scoop"
    Pruitt), Jimmy Boyd (Robert Higgson), Gavin MacLeod (Professor Thayer),
    Kenneth MacKenna (President Byrne of Pinehurst), Nina Shipman (Laura
    Howard), Angus Duncan (Harvey Howard Jr.), Carla Borelli (Harvey Jr.'s
    date), Alvin Childress (Guest Announcer), Douglass Dumbrille (Judge Carter)
Color, 103 minutes

BREAKFAST AT TIFFANY'S (1961)
Paramount Pictures
Producer: Martin Jurow, Richard Shepherd
Director: **Blake Edwards**
Screenplay: George Axelrod (based on *Breakfast at Tiffany's* by Truman Capote)
Cinematography: Franz F. Planer, Philip H. Lathrop (uncredited)
Editing: Howard Smith
Music: Henry Mancini
Cast: Audrey Hepburn (Holly Golightly/Lula Mae Barnes), George Peppard (Paul "Fred" Varjak), Patricia Neal (Mrs. Emily Eustace "2E" Failenson), Buddy Ebsen (Doc Golightly), Martin Balsam (O. J. Berman), Mickey Rooney (I. Y. Yunioshi), Alan Reed (Sally Tomato), José Luis de Vilallonga (José da Silva Pereira), Stanley Adams (Rutherford "Rusty" Trawler), John McGiver (Tiffany's salesman), Orangey (Cat, trained by Frank Inn), Elvia Allman (Librarian), Mel Blanc (Holly's over-eager date, uncredited)
Color, 114 minutes

EXPERIMENT IN TERROR (1962)
Columbia Pictures
Producer: **Blake Edwards**
Director: **Blake Edwards**
Screenplay: Mildred Gordon, Gordon Gordon
Cinematography: Philip H. Lathrop
Editing: Patrick McCormack
Music: Henry Mancini
Cast: Glenn Ford (John "Rip" Ripley), Lee Remick (Kelly Sherwood), Stefanie Powers (Toby Sherwood), Ross Martin (Garland Humphrey "Red" Lynch), Ned Glass (Popcorn), Clifton James (Capt. Moreno), William Bryant (Chuck), Dick Crockett (FBI Agent #1), James Lanphier (Landlord), Clarence Lung (Attorney Yung)
B&W, 123 minutes

DAYS OF WINE AND ROSES (1962)
Warner Bros.
Producer: Martin Manulis
Director: **Blake Edwards**
Screenplay: JP Miller
Cinematography: Philip H. Lathrop
Editing: Patrick McCormack
Music: Henry Mancini

Cast: Jack Lemmon (Joe Clay), Lee Remick (Kirsten Arnesen Clay), Charles Bickford (Ellis Arnesen), Jack Klugman (Jim Hungerford), Alan Hewitt (Rad Leland), Tom Palmer (Ballefoy), Debbie Megowan (Debbie Clay), Maxine Stuart (Dottie), Jack Albertson (Trayner), Ken Lynch (Liquor Store Proprietor), Mel Blanc (TV Cartoon Characters' voices), Jack Riley (Waiter), Katherine Squire (Mrs. Nolan), Jennifer Edwards (Debbie Clay at age 5), Lynn Borden (Party Guest, uncredited)

B&W, 117 minutes

THE PINK PANTHER (1963)
United Artists
Producer: Martin Jurow
Director: **Blake Edwards**
Screenplay: Maurice Richlin, **Blake Edwards**
Cinematography: Philip Lathrop
Editing: Ralph E. Winters
Music: Henry Mancini
Cast: David Niven (Sir Charles Lytton), Peter Sellers (Inspector Jacques Clouseau), Robert Wagner (George Lytton), Capucine (Simone Clouseau), Claudia Cardinale (Princess Dala; Gale Garnett, uncredited voice), Brenda De Banzie (Angela Dunning), Colin Gordon (Tucker), John Le Mesurier (Defense Attorney), James Lanphier (Saloud), Michael Trubshawe (Felix Townes), Riccardo Billi (Aristotle Sarajos), Martin Miller (Pierre Luigi), Fran Jeffries (Ski Lodge Singer)

Color, 113 minutes

A SHOT IN THE DARK (1964)
United Artists
Producer: **Blake Edwards**
Director: **Blake Edwards**
Screenplay: **Blake Edwards**, William Peter Blatty
Cinematography: Christopher Challis
Editing: Bert Bates, Ralph E. Winters
Music: Henry Mancini
Cast: Peter Sellers (Jacques Clouseau), Elke Sommer (Maria Gambrelli), George Sanders (Benjamin Ballon), Herbert Lom (Charles Dreyfus), Tracy Reed (Dominique Ballon), Graham Stark (Hercule Lajoy), Moira Redmond (Simone), Vanda Godsell (Madame LaFarge), Maurice Kaufmann (Pierre), Ann Lynn (Dudu), David Lodge (Georges), André Maranne (François), Martin Benson (Maurice), Burt Kwouk (Cato), Reginald Beckwith (Receptionist), Douglas

Wilmer (Henri LaFarge), Bryan Forbes (Camp Attendant, credited as Turk Thrust), Jack Melford (The Psycho-Analyst)

Color, 102 minutes

THE GREAT RACE (1965)
Warner Bros.
Producer: Martin Jurow
Director: **Blake Edwards**
Screenplay: Arthur A. Ross
Story: **Blake Edwards**, Arthur A. Ross
Cinematography: Russell Harlan
Editing: Ralph E. Winters
Music: Henry Mancini
Cast: Jack Lemmon (Professor Fate/Prince Friedrich Hapnick), Tony Curtis (Leslie Gallant III), Natalie Wood (Maggie DuBois), Peter Falk (Maximillian "Max" Meen), Keenan Wynn (Hezekiah Sturdy), Arthur O'Connell (Henry Goodbody), Vivian Vance (Hester Goodbody), Dorothy Provine (Lily Olay), Larry Storch (Texas Jack), Ross Martin (Baron Rolfe von Stuppe), Hal Smith (Mayor of Boracho), Denver Pyle (Sheriff of Boracho), Marvin Kaplan (Frisbee), George Macready (General Kuhster), Joyce Nizzari (Woman in West), Ken Wales (Baron's Guard), William Bryant (Baron's Guard)
Color, 160 minutes

WHAT DID YOU DO IN THE WAR, DADDY? (1966)
United Artists
Producer: **Blake Edwards**
Director: **Blake Edwards**
Screenplay: William Peter Blatty
Story: Maurice Richlin, **Blake Edwards**
Cinematography: Philip H. Lathrop
Editing: Ralph E. Winters
Music: Ray Evans, Jay Livingston, Henry Mancini
Cast: James Coburn (Lieutenant Jody Christian), Dick Shawn (Captain Lionel Cash), Sergio Fantoni (Captain Fausto Oppo), Giovanna Ralli (Gina Romano), Aldo Ray (Sergeant Rizzo), Harry Morgan (Major Pott), Carroll O'Connor (General Max Bolt), Leon Askin (Colonel Kastorp), Rico Cattani (Benedetto), Jay Novello (Mayor Giuseppe Romano), Ralph Manza (Waiter), Vito Scotti (Frederico), Johnny Seven (Vittorio), Art Lewis (Needleman), William Bryant (Minow), Kurt Kreuger (German Captain)
Color, 116 minutes

GUNN (1967)
Paramount Pictures
Producer: Owen Crump, **Blake Edwards**
Director: **Blake Edwards**
Screenplay: William Peter Blatty, **Blake Edwards**
Story: **Blake Edwards**
Cinematography: Philip Lathrop
Music: The Gordian Knot, Henry Mancini
Cast: Craig Stevens (Peter Gunn), Laura Devon (Edie), Edward Asner (Jacoby),
Albert Paulsen (Fusco), Helen Traubel (Mother), Regis Toomey (The Bishop),
J. Pat O'Malley (Tinker), Sherry Jackson (Samantha)
Color, 94 minutes

THE PARTY (1968)
United Artists
Producer: **Blake Edwards**
Director: **Blake Edwards**
Screenplay: **Blake Edwards**, Tom Waldman, Frank Waldman (based on story by
Blake Edwards)
Cinematography: Lucien Ballard
Editing: Ralph E. Winters
Music: Henry Mancini
Cast: Peter Sellers (Hrundi V. Bakshi), Claudine Longet (Michele Monet), Natalia
Borisova (Ballerina), Jean Carson (Nanny), Marge Champion (Rosalind Dun-
phy), Al Checco (Bernard Stein), Corinne Cole (Janice Kane), Dick Crockett
(Walls), Danielle de Metz (Stella D'Angelo), Herb Ellis (Charlie), Paul Ferr-
ara (Ronald "Ronnie" Smith), Steve Franken (Levinson), Kathe Green (Molly
Clutterbuck), James Lanphier (Harry), Buddy Lester (Davey Kane), Gavin
MacLeod (C. S. Divot), Fay McKenzie (Alice Clutterbuck), J. Edward McKinley
(General Fred R. Clutterbuck), Denny Miller (William "Wyoming Bill" Kelso),
Timothy Scott (Gore Pontoon), Carol Wayne (June Warren), Helen Kleeb
(Secretary), Linda Gaye Scott (Starlet)
Color, 99 minutes

DARLING LILI (1970)
Paramount Pictures
Producer: **Blake Edwards**
Director: **Blake Edwards**
Screenplay: William Peter Blatty, **Blake Edwards**
Cinematography: Russell Harlan

Editing: Peter Zinner
Music: Henry Mancini, Johnny Mercer (lyrics)
Cast: Julie Andrews (Lili Smith/Schmidt), Rock Hudson (Mayor William Larra-
bee), Jeremy Kemp (Colonel Kurt Von Ruger), Lance Percival (Lieutenant
Carstairs), Michael Witney (Youngblood Carson), Jacques Marin (Duvalle),
André Maranne (Lieutenant Liggett), Gloria Paul (Crepe Suzette), Bernard
Kay (Bedford), Doreen Keogh (Emma)
Color, 136 minutes (107 minutes, director's cut; 190 minutes, original roadshow
release)

WILD ROVERS (1971)
Metro-Goldwyn-Mayer
Producer: **Blake Edwards**, Ken Wales
Director: **Blake Edwards**
Screenplay: **Blake Edwards**
Cinematography: Philip Lathrop
Editing: John F. Burnett
Music: Jerry Goldsmith
Cast: William Holden (Ross Bodine), Ryan O'Neal (Frank Post), Karl Malden (Walt
Buckman), Joe Don Baker (Paul Buckman), Tom Skerritt (John Buckman),
James Olson (Joe Billings), Lynn Carlin (Sada Billings), Leora Dana (Nell
Buckman), Victor French (Sheriff Bill Jackson), Rachel Roberts (Maybell
Tucker)
Color, 136 minutes

THE CAREY TREATMENT (1972)
Metro-Goldwyn-Mayer
Producer: William Belasco
Director: **Blake Edwards**
Screenplay: James P. Bonner
Cinematography: Frank Stanley
Music: Roy Budd
Cast: James Coburn (Dr. Peter Carey), Jennifer O'Neill (Georgia Hightower), Pat
Hingle (Capt. Pearson), Skye Aubrey (Nurse Angela Holder), Elizabeth Allen
(Evelyn Randall), John Fink (Chief Surgeon Andrew Murphy), Dan O'Herlihy
(J. D. Randall), James Hong (David Tao), Alex Dreier (Dr. Joshua Randall),
Michael Blodgett (Roger Hudson), Regis Toomey (Sanderson the Pathologist),
Steve Carlson (Walding), Rosemary Edelman (Janet Tao), Jennifer Edwards
(Lydia Barrett), John Hillerman (Jenkins)
Color, 101 minutes

THE TAMARIND SEED (1974)
Avco Embassy Pictures
Producer: Ken Wales
Director: **Blake Edwards**
Screenplay: **Blake Edwards** (based on *The Tamarind Seed* by Evelyn Anthony)
Cinematography: Freddie Young
Editing: Ernest Walter
Music: John Barry
Cast: Julie Andrews (Judith Farrow), Omar Sharif (Feodor Sverdlov), Anthony
    Quayle (Jack Loder), Dan O'Herlihy (Fergus Stephenson), Sylvia Syms (Mar-
    garet Stephenson), Oskar Homolka (General Golitsyn), Bryan Marshall
    (George MacLeod), David Baron (Richard Paterson), Celia Bannerman (Rachel
    Paterson), Roger Dann (Col. Moreau), Sharon Duce (Sandy Mitchell), George
    Mikell (Maj. Stukalov), Kate O'Mara (Anna Skriabina), Constantine Gregory
    (Dimitri Memenov)
Color, 119 minutes

THE RETURN OF THE PINK PANTHER (1975)
United Artists
Producer: **Blake Edwards**
Director: **Blake Edwards**
Screenplay: Frank Waldman, **Blake Edwards**
Cinematography: Geoffrey Unsworth
Editing: Tom Priestly
Music: Henry Mancini
Cast: Peter Sellers (Inspector Jacques Clouseau), Herbert Lom (Chief Inspector
    Charles Dreyfus), Christopher Plummer (Sir Charles Litton), Catherine Schell
    (Lady Claudine Litton), Burt Kwouk (Cato Fong), Peter Arne (Colonel Sharki),
    Peter Jeffrey (General Wadafi), Grégoire Aslan (Chief of Lugash Police), Da-
    vid Lodge (Mac), Graham Stark (Pepi), Eric Pohlmann (The Fat Man), André
    Maranne (François), Victor Spinetti (Hotel Concierge), John Bluthal (Blind
    Beggar), Mike Grady (Bell Boy), Peter Jones (Psychiatrist)
Color, 114 minutes

THE PINK PANTHER STRIKES AGAIN (1976)
United Artists
Producer: **Blake Edwards**, Tony Adams (associate)
Director: **Blake Edwards**
Screenplay: Frank Waldman, **Blake Edwards**
Cinematography: Harry Waxman

Editing: Alan Jones

Music: Henry Mancini

Cast: Peter Sellers (Chief Inspector Jacques Clouseau), Herbert Lom (Former Chief Inspector Charles Dreyfus), Leonard Rossiter (Superintendent Quinlan), Lesley-Anne Down (Olga Bariosova), Colin Blakely (Inspector Alec Drummond), Burt Kwouk (Cato Fong), André Maranne (Sgt. François Chevalier), Michael Robbins (Ainsley Jarvis), Richard Vernon (Professor Hugo Fassbender), Briony McRoberts (Margo Fassbender), Dick Crockett (President of the United States), Byron Kane (US Secretary of State), Gordon Rollings (Inmate), Dudley Sutton (Inspector Mclaren)

Color, 103 minutes

REVENGE OF THE PINK PANTHER (1978)

United Artists

Producer: **Blake Edwards**

Director: **Blake Edwards**

Screenplay: Frank Waldman, Ron Clark, **Blake Edwards**

Story: **Blake Edwards**

Cinematography: Ernest Day

Editing: Alan Jones

Music: Henry Mancini, Leslie Bricusse (songwriter)

Cast: Peter Sellers (Chief Inspector Jacques Clouseau), Herbert Lom (Chief Inspector Charles Dreyfus), Dyan Cannon (Simone Legree), Robert Webber (Philippe Douvier), Paul Stewart (Julio Scallini), Burt Kwouk (Cato Fong), Tony Beckley (Guy Algo), Robert Loggia (Al Marchione), André Maranne (Sgt. François Chevalier), Graham Stark (Prof. Auguste Balls), Alfie Bass (Fernet), Sue Lloyd (Claude Russo), Danny Schiller (Cunny), Douglas Wilmer (Police Commissioner), Ferdy Mayne (Dr. Paul Laprone), Valerie Leon (Tanya), Ed Parker (Mr. Chong, uncredited), Adrienne Corri (Therese Douvier), Henry McGee (Officer Bardot), Andrew Sachs (Hercule Poirot), Julian Orchard (Hospital Clerk), John Bluthal (Guard at Cemetery), Rita Webb (Woman at Window)

Color, 98 minutes

10 (1979)

Warner Bros.

Producer: **Blake Edwards**, Tony Adams

Director: **Blake Edwards**

Screenplay: **Blake Edwards**

Cinematography: Frank Stanley

Editing: Ralph E. Winters

Music: Henry Mancini
Cast: Dudley Moore (George Webber), Julie Andrews (Samantha Taylor), Bo Derek (Jenny Hanley), Robert Webber (Hugh), Dee Wallace (Mary Lewis), Sam J. Jones (David Hanley), Brian Dennehy (Don the Bartender), Max Showalter (Reverend), Burke Byrnes (as Himself)
Color, 122 minutes

S.O.B. (1981)
Paramount Pictures
Producer: Tony Adams, **Blake Edwards**
Director: **Blake Edwards**
Screenplay: **Blake Edwards**
Cinematography: Harry Stradling Jr.
Editing: Ralph E. Winters
Music: Henry Mancini
Cast: Julie Andrews (Sally Miles), William Holden (Tim Culley), Marisa Berenson (Mavis), Larry Hagman (Dick Benson), Robert Loggia (Herb Maskowitz), Stuart Margolin (Gary Murdock), Richard Mulligan (Felix Farmer), Robert Preston (Dr. Irving Finegarten), Craig Stevens (Willard), Loretta Swit (Polly Reed), Robert Vaughn (David Blackman), Robert Webber (Ben Coogan), Shelley Winters (Eva Brown), Jennifer Edwards (Lila), Rosanna Arquette (Babs), John Pleshette (Capitol Studios Vice President), John Lawlor (Capitol Studios Manager), Ken Swofford (Harold P. Harrigan), Hamilton Camp (Lipschitz), Paul Stewart (Harry Sandler), Benson Fong (Personal Chef), Larry Storch (Swami), Virginia Gregg (Funeral Director's Wife), Joe Penny (Officer Buchwald), Erica Yohn (Agnes), Colleen Brennan (Tammy Taylor), Gene Nelson (Blive Lytell), Charles Lampkin (Butler), Corbin Bernsen (Surfer on Beach)
Color, 122 minutes

VICTOR/VICTORIA (1982)
Metro-Goldwyn-Mayer
Producer: Tony Adams, **Blake Edwards**
Director: **Blake Edwards**
Screenplay: **Blake Edwards**, Hans Hoemburg (concept) (based on a 1933 script by Reinhold Schünzel)
Cinematography: Dick Bush
Editing: Ralph E. Winters
Music: Henry Mancini, Leslie Bricusse (lyrics)
Cast: Julie Andrews (Victoria Grant/Count Victor Grazinki), James Garner (King Marchand), Robert Preston (Carroll "Toddy" Todd), Lesley Ann Warren

(Norma Cassidy), Alex Karras ("Squash" Bernstein), John Rhys-Davies (Andre Cassell), Graham Stark (Waiter), Peter Arne (Labisse), Malcolm Jamieson (Richard Di Nardo), Sherloque Tanney (Charles Bovin), Michael Robbins (Manager of Victoria's Hotel), Maria Charles (Madame President), Glen Murphy (Boxer), Geoffrey Beevers (Police Inspector), Norman Alden (Man in Hotel with Shoes, uncredited), Jay Benedict (Guy Longois)
Color, 132 minutes

TRAIL OF THE PINK PANTHER (1982)
MGM/UA Entertainment Company
Producer: **Blake Edwards**, Tony Adams
Director: **Blake Edwards**
Screenplay: Frank Waldman, Tom Waldman, **Blake Edwards**, Geoffrey Edwards
Story: **Blake Edwards**
Cinematography: Dick Bush
Editing: Alan Jones
Music: Henry Mancini
Cast: Peter Sellers (Inspector Jacques Clouseau, archival footage only), David Niven (Sir Charles Litton), Herbert Lom (Chief Inspector Charles Dreyfus), Burt Kwouk (Cato Fong), Richard Mulligan (Clouseau's Father), Joanna Lumley (Marie Jouveat), Capucine (Lady Simone Litton), Robert Loggia (Bruno Langois), Harvey Korman (Prof. Auguste Balls), André Maranne (Sgt. François Chevalier), Graham Stark (Hercule Lajoy), Daniel Peacock (Clouseau, age 18), Lucca Mezzofanti (Clouseau, age 8), Colin Blakely (Alec Drummond), Denise Crosby (Denise, Bruno's moll)
Color, 96 minutes

CURSE OF THE PINK PANTHER (1983)
MGM/UA Entertainment Company
Producer: **Blake Edwards**, Tony Adams
Director: **Blake Edwards**
Screenplay: **Blake Edwards**, Geoffrey Edwards
Cinematography: Dick Bush
Editing: Robert Hathaway, Ralph E. Winters
Music: Henry Mancini
Cast: David Niven (Sir Charles Litton), Ted Wass (Sgt. Clifton Sleigh), Herbert Lom (Chief Inspector Charles Dreyfus), Robert Loggia (Bruno Langois), Joanna Lumley (Countess Chandra), Capucine (Lady Simone Litton), Robert Wagner (George Litton), Burt Kwouk (Cato Fong), Leslie Ash (Juleta Shane), André Maranne (François), Ed Parker (Mr. Chong), Bill Nighy (ENT Doctor),

Roger Moore (Inspector Jacques Clouseau, billed as Turk Thrust II), Harvey Korman (Prof. Auguste Balls), Liz Smith (Martha), Michael Elphick (Valencia Police Chief), Hugh Fraser (Dr. Stang), Joe Morton (Charlie), Denise Crosby (Denise, Bruno's moll)
Color, 109 minutes

THE MAN WHO LOVED WOMEN (1983)
Columbia Pictures
Producer: Tony Adams, **Blake Edwards**
Director: **Blake Edwards**
Screenplay: **Blake Edwards**, Milton Wexler, Geoffrey Edwards
Story: Michel Fermaud, Suzanne Schiffman, François Truffaut
Cinematography: Haskell Wexler
Editing: Ralph E. Winters
Music: Henry Mancini
Cast: Burt Reynolds (David Fowler), Julie Andrews (Marianna), Kim Basinger (Louise), Marilu Henner (Agnes), Cynthia Sikes (Courtney), Jennifer Edwards (Nancy), Sela Ward (Janet), Ellen Bauer (Svetlana), Denise Crosby (Enid), Tracy Vaccaro (Legs), Barry Corbin (Roy), Roger Rose (Sergeant Stone)
Color, 110 minutes

MICKI AND MAUDE (1984)
Columbia Pictures
Producer: Tony Adams
Director: **Blake Edwards**
Screenplay: Jonathan Reynolds
Cinematography: Harry Stradling Jr.
Editing: Ralph E. Winters
Music: Lee Holdridge
Cast: Ann Reinking (Micki), Amy Irving (Maude Guillory), Dudley Moore (Rob Salinger), Richard Mulligan (Leo), George Gaynes (Dr. Glztszki), Wallace Shawn (Dr. Fibel), Hard Boiled Haggerty (Barkhas Guillory), John Pleshette (Hap Ludlow), Andre Rousimmoff (Wrestler), Lu Leonard (Nurse Verbeck), Roger Rose (Newscaster)
Color, 118 minutes

A FINE MESS (1986)
Columbia Pictures
Producer: Tony Adams
Director: **Blake Edwards**

Screenplay: **Blake Edwards**
Cinematography: Harry Stradling Jr.
Music: Henry Mancini
Cast: Ted Danson (Spence Holden), Howie Mandel (Dennis Powell), Richard Mulligan (Wayne "Turnip" Parragella), Stuart Margolin (Maurice "Binky" Drundza), María Conchita Alonso (Claudia Pazzo), Jennifer Edwards (Ellen Frankenthaler), Paul Sorvino (Tony Pazzo), Rick Ducommun (Wardell), Keye Luke (Ishimine), Ed Herlihy (TV Reporter), Walter Charles (Auctioneer), Tawny Moyer (Leading Lady), Emma Walton (First Extra), Carrie Leigh (Second Extra), Sharan Lea (Young Girl), Dennis Franz (Phil), Larry Storch (Leopold Klop)
Color, 90 minutes

THAT'S LIFE (1986)
Columbia Pictures
Producer: Tony Adams, Jonathan D. Krane
Director: **Blake Edwards**
Screenplay: **Blake Edwards**, Milton Wexler
Cinematography: Anthony B. Richmond
Music: Henry Mancini
Cast: Jack Lemmon (Harvey Fairchild), Julie Andrews (Gillian Fairchild), Sally Kellerman (Holly Parrish), Robert Loggia (Father Baragone), Jennifer Edwards (Megan Fairchild Bartlet), Rob Knepper (Steve Larwin), Matt Lattanzi (Larry Bartlet), Chris Lemmon (Josh Fairchild), Cynthia Sikes (Janice Kern), Dana Sparks (Fanny Ward), Emma Walton (Kate Fairchild), Felicia Farr (Madame Carrie), Theodore Wilson (Corey), Nicky Blair (Andre), Jordan Christopher (Dr. Keith Romanis), Biff Elliot (Belmont), Hal Riddle (Phil Carlson), Harold Harris (Harold), Sherry P. Sievert (Receptionist), Dr. Charles Schneider (Dr. Gerald Spelner)
Color, 102 minutes

BLIND DATE (1987)
TriStar Pictures
Producer: Tony Adams
Director: **Blake Edwards**
Screenplay: Dale Launer
Cinematography: Harry Stradling Jr.
Editing: Robert Pergament
Music: Henry Mancini
Cast: Bruce Willis (Walter Davis), Kim Basinger (Nadia Gates), John Larroquette

(David Bedford), William Daniels (Judge Harold Bedford), George Coe (Harry Gruen), Mark Blum (Denny Gordon), Phil Hartman (Ted Davis), Stephanie Faracy (Susie Davis), Alice Hirson (Muriel Bedford), Stanley Jordan (as himself), Graham Stark (Jordan the Butler), Joyce Van Patten (Nadia's Mother), Barry Sobel (Gas Station Attendant), Armin Shimerman (French Waiter), Brian George (Maitre d'), Dick Durock (Bouncer), Sab Shimono (Mr. Yakamoto), Momo Yashima (Mrs. Yakamoto), Herb Tanney (Minister)
Color, 95 minutes

SUNSET (1988)
TriStar Pictures
Producer: Tony Adams
Director: **Blake Edwards**
Screenplay: **Blake Edwards**
Cinematography: Anthony B. Richmond
Editing: Robert Pergament
Music: Henry Mancini
Cast: Bruce Willis (Tom Mix), James Garner (Wyatt Earp), Malcolm McDowell (Alfie Alperin), Mariel Hemingway (Cheryl King), Kathleen Quinlan (Nancy Shoemaker), Jennifer Edwards (Victoria Alperin), Patricia Hodge (Christina Alperin), Richard Bradford (Capt. Blackworth), M. Emmet Walsh (Chief Dibner), Joe Dallesandro (Dutch Kieffer), Andreas Katsulas (Arthur), Dann Florek (Marty Goldberg), Bill Marcus (Hal Flynn), Michael C. Gwynne (Mooch), Dermot Mulroney (Michael Alperin), Jeffrey Briar (Stan Laurel), Bevis Faversham (Oliver Hardy), John Fountain (John Gilbert), Peter Jason (Frank Coe), Darrah Meeley (Reporter)
Color, 103 minutes

SKIN DEEP (1989)
20th Century Fox
Producer: Tony Adams, James G. Robinson (executive), Joe Roth (co-producer)
Director: **Blake Edwards**
Screenplay: **Blake Edwards**
Cinematography: Isidore Mankofsky
Editing: Robert Pergament
Music: Don Grady, Henry Mancini, Ivan Neville
Cast: John Ritter (Zachary "Zach" Hutton), Vincent Gardenia (Barney the Barkeeper), Alyson Reed (Alexandra "Alex" Hutton), Joel Brooks (Jake Fedderman), Julianne Phillips (Molly), Chelsea Field (Amy McKenna), Peter Donat (Leon "Sparky" Sparks), Don Gordon (Curt Ames), Nina Foch (Marge, Alex's

Mother), Denise Crosby (Angela "Angie" Smith), Michael Kidd (Dr. Westford), Dee Dee Rescher (Bernice Fedderman), Bryan Genesse (Rick Curry), Bo Foxworth (Greg), Ray Hollitt (Lonnie Jones), Brenda Swanson (Emily), Jean Marie McKee (Rebecca "Becky")
Color, 97 minutes

SWITCH (1991)
Warner Bros. (Time Warner)
Producer: Tony Adams, Arnon Milchan (executive), Patrick Wachsberg (executive), Trish Caroselli (associate)
Director: **Blake Edwards**
Screenplay: **Blake Edwards**
Cinematography: Dick Bush
Editing: Robert Pergament
Music: Henry Mancini, Don Grady
Cast: Ellen Barkin (Amanda Brooks), Jimmy Smits (Walter Stone), JoBeth Williams (Margo Brofman), Lorraine Bracco (Sheila Faxton), Tony Roberts (Arnold Freidkin), Perry King (Steve Brooks), Bruce Payne (The Devil), Lysette Anthony (Liz), Victoria Mahoney (Felicia), Basil Hoffman (Higgins), Catherine Keener (Steve's Secretary), Kevin Kilner (Dan Jones), David Wohl (Attorney Caldwell), James Harper (Lt. Laster), John Lafayette (Sgt. Phillips), Téa Leoni (Connie the Dream Girl)
Color, 103 minutes

SON OF THE PINK PANTHER (1993)
Metro-Goldwyn-Mayer/United Artists
Producer: Tony Adams
Director: **Blake Edwards**
Screenplay: **Blake Edwards**, Madeline Sunshine, Steve Sunshine
Story: **Blake Edwards** (based on characters by **Blake Edwards** and Maurice Richlin)
Cinematography: Dick Bush
Editing: Robert Pergament
Music: Henry Mancini
Cast: Roberto Benigni (Gendarme Jacques Gambrelli), Herbert Lom (Commissioner Charles Dreyfus), Claudia Cardinale (Maria), Debrah Farentino (Princess Yasmin), Jennifer Edwards (Yussa), Robert Davi (Hans Zarba), Mark Schneider (Arnon), Burt Kwouk (Cato Fong), Mike Starr (Hanif), Kenny Spalding (Garth), Anton Rodgers (Chief Lazar), Graham Stark (Professor Auguste Balls), Oliver Cotton (King Haroak), Shabana Azmi (Queen), Aharon

Ipalé (Gen. Jaffar), Dermot Crowley (Sergeant François Duval), Liz Smith (Marta Balls),
Color, 93 minutes

Blake Edwards: Interviews

The Edwardian Look

Joe Hyams / 1959

From *New York Herald Tribune*, November 29, 1959, pp. 60–62. Reprinted by permission of the Dolph Briscoe Center for American History (Austin, Texas).

Have you ever wondered who is the pattern for most of the private eyes on television? Well, I went to interview Blake Edwards, the man who created *Peter Gunn*, *Richard Diamond*, and the current *Mr. Lucky*. Edwards was reluctant to tell me who the prototype was—but he didn't fool me for a minute. Blake Edwards is not only the creator, he is also the prototype.

Consider the facts: Edwards is in his middle thirties, is six feet tall, dresses extremely well, is married to a beautiful girl, drives a Mercedes Benz, is well up on judo, and is a mystery story fan and a jazz aficionado. Edwards might well have been writing about himself when he created *Peter Gunn*. In fact, he even took Craig Stevens—Peter—to his tailor and had him outfitted in the same clothes Edwards wears.

Although it seems to me that Edwards and Peter Gunn, et al., are one and the same, apparently one of the reasons the private eye shows are so popular is that the home viewer believes that "he" is the hero, too. Psychiatrists and others call this identification and all the "eye" shows seem to feature an inordinate amount of it.

As Edwards sees it, "The guy at home is sitting in front of his TV set surrounded by wife, kids, and responsibility, but he likes to imagine himself a lady-killer, a guy from everywhere, an omnipotent man free to do what he wants, say what he thinks, and think what he wants."

This identification can be used in two ways. There are "guys at home" who also identify with the criminal rather than with the hero. Dr. Ernst Dichter of the Institute for Motivation and Research believes it possible that many viewers identify more with the criminal, hoping he, not the private eye, will win out, and he wonders, as do I, if a show where the criminal is the hero wouldn't be just as popular.

This is a theory which Edwards has considered before, and there are elements of gangsterism—on a socially acceptable level, of course—in all the shows he has created. For example, Gunn and Diamond are not averse to illegally breaking and entering a home in the interest of justice, and Mr. Lucky is a professional gambler.

The world of the private detective, as well as the cowboy's world, is one in which justice is the result of direct action, not of elaborate legality.

Explaining the tremendous amount of violence in his shows Edwards noted, "Sometimes a man gets into a situation where the only thing he can do is to fight his way out with his fists." He added, "The audience demands this kind of situation."

It seems to me that regardless of how far from reality these private eyes browse, they are entitled to as much poetic and dramatic license as the Westerns, the fantasies of the TV tube being merely reflections of the larger drama.

Says Edwards, "The job the private eye has to do on television is the kind of thing the audience would feel they could never get mixed up in, like murder or robbery. It's all right to have a man identify as long as he's living vicariously. But if you get involved in something he is familiar with, he suddenly decides to become a critic."

As Edwards talked, I was reminded of what John Crosby wrote recently—"All the private eyes seem to be imitating somebody, mostly Cary Grant."

Edwards did indeed remind me of someone, namely Mr. Grant. The fact is, all the heroes bear a remarkable resemblance to Grant (and Edwards). Craig Stevens (Peter Gunn) is thirty-eight years old, 6'2", weighs 180 pounds; David Janssen (Richard Diamond) is twenty-nine, 6'1", 195 pounds; John Vivyan is thirty-six, 6'3", 195 pounds; Efrem Zimbalist Jr. (Stu Bailey of 77 *Sunset Strip*) is thirty-five, 6', 170 pounds. Cary Grant is fifty-six years old, but is 6'1", weighs 174, and Edwards is thirty-eight, 6'1", 175.

I asked Edwards why none of the private eyes seem able to endure or sustain a real romance with a female. Peter Gunn, for example, is notable for the number of times he gets up to bat with Edie (Lola Albright) only to foul out at the lady's first pitch.

"It's necessary to be unattached," said Edwards, who also directs the show. "Involvement means attachment to the guy at home who'd generally rather walk out on a girl than give her a tumble. Thus his ego remains secure."

In that one area alone Edwards and his hero-projections part company. He is a happily married man and a father. Otherwise the shoe—or the expensive sports car—fits him mighty well indeed.

All Set

Show / 1962

From *Show*, May 1962.

Two blonde Amazons swung dangerously back and forth on trapezes suspended high above the bar. Stale cigarette smoke filled the red plush room, although it was still early morning. "When do we get a coffee break?" a puffy-eyed bit player whispered to a grip. "Can't we have a little damn quiet? We're shooting!" cried an exasperated assistant director. "Isn't she sweet?" said a middle-aged woman extra to no one in particular, referring to actress Lee Remick, who was sitting at the bar under klieg lights, peering anxiously into the crowded dark around her. The setting was San Francisco's much-touted Roaring Twenties nightclub, where Miss Remick has her first rendezvous with a murderer in *Experiment in Terror*.

"Okay, ten-minute break," shouted Blake Edwards, the director. Edwards, a boyish man in his late thirties with a tight blond crew cut, watched his star head for the coffee wagon. "I'm mad about Lee," he said. "She's just great, a really instinctive actress. This is the first suspense I've filmed since I stopped doing *Peter Gunn* on television. I've been making comedies. *Operation Petticoat* and then *Breakfast at Tiffany's*. I don't really care much about what kind of film I do. Life doesn't go in a straight line. But I get awfully involved with whatever I'm doing at the moment.

"I think audiences go to suspense films for escape and enjoyment. That's why you won't see a lot of obvious violence in *Experiment*. That's too easy. The violence is always just under the surface, waiting. And, above all, in this kind of film, you've got to heighten the horror by contrasting it with the everyday world. That's why we're filming it all here in San Francisco. Lee, of course, is perfect for the part. Can you think of a more apple-pie-normal heroine to tie to the railroad tracks?"

Miss Remick returned. "I'm just mad about Blake. I've had good luck with movie directors," she said, "but he's my favorite. I made my debut with Gadg Kazan [*A Face in the Crowd*], and he's one of the kindest men I ever knew. Marty Ritt [*The Long, Hot Summer*] too, even if he did say once that I was a kind of 'healthy American peasant.'"

She laughed. "Preminger scared me to death at first. I'd heard a lot of awful rumors about him before I went to do *Anatomy of a Murder*, but he was always a gentleman with me. With Blake, I'm closer. We're producing this movie together, you know. It's called a Geoffrey-Kate Production, after his son and my daughter. And when we're finished, why then we'll do one more together, *Days of Wine and Roses*, in San Francisco again.

"I love movies, but I don't make one right after the other, as a rule. I plan my pictures around having babies. The values have changed out here. Actresses didn't used to just run off and have children when they wanted to. The studios dictated their lives. I'm afraid we were more interesting to the public then. There's nothing much to print about my daily life—no divorces, no whoop-de-do." A woman with needle and thread took Miss Remick's arm and went to work on a loose button.

"Are you ready, Mr. Edwards?" a demure voice asked from above. Edwards looked up to the girls on the trapezes, consulted his watch, and called out to the set: "Okay, let's go, Lee." Miss Remick got up on her stool again and blinked at the hot klieg lights, the crowd grew silent, and the blondes swung on.

Blake Edwards:
Busted Budgets Are Box Office

Louella and Harriet Parsons / 1965

From *New York Journal-American*, June 20, 1965. Reprinted by permission of Hearst/William Van Niekerken, Library Director, *San Francisco Chronicle*.

Forty-two-year old writer-producer-director-ex-actor Blake Edwards, whose $12,000,000 epic farce, *The Great Race*, stars Jack Lemmon, Tony Curtis, and Natalie Wood, is rated one of Hollywood's most individual and creative talents. He also ranks among the town's top money-makers. Warner Brothers, for whom he made *The Great Race* on a marathon schedule which brought him to blows with bossman Jack Warner, now thinks the wild and woolly fun-fest may turn out to be the biggest comedy money-maker of all time. Considering the cost, it better.

It's understandable that studios would be a little nervous about hiring the ruggedly individual, budget-ignoring young genius. *Great Race* was shopped around quite a bit before it landed at Warners. But his track record can't be argued with—hits like *Pink Panther*, *A Shot in the Dark*, *Breakfast at Tiffany's*, and *Operation Petticoat*—plus *Peter Gunn* on TV.

After examining the figures the Mirisch Brothers recently signed him to a six-film, $20-million production deal. His first on the new set-up will be *What Did You Do in the War, Daddy?*, a World War II comedy. The locale is Italy, but Blake will build an entire Italian city near Lake Sherwood outside Hollywood.

Blake is used to spending money. He recalls, "Columbia once let me go because I went six days over on a fifteen-day schedule. I didn't set out to go over schedule—I set out to make the best picture I could. Anyway, I think studio schedules and budgets are usually unrealistic, anyway. At Universal I ran over on *Operation Petticoat*, and by the time the picture was released I was out of the studio!" (*Operation Petticoat* turned out to be one of the biggest grossers in the studio's history.)

"Then on *Breakfast at Tiffany's* at Paramount," Blake went on, "they panicked because I took eight days to shoot the party scene and insisted on actors instead of extras." (The party scene was one of the highlights of *Tiffany's*—which made lots of money, too.)

He's been associated largely with comedy, but Blake also has to his credit the heart-breaking *Days of Wine and Roses* and the thriller, *Experiment in Terror.*

As colorful as he is talented, Edwards has many facets. He collects guns and chessmen and also has an impressive array of paintings in his big, comfortable Holmby Hills house. He's an expert of karate and also yoga. He says that he practices yoga exercises every day—even on the set. "I find it helps when that four o'clock sag sets in."

Next to wife Patty and their kids, eight-year-old Jennifer and five-year-old Geoffrey, his greatest love is probably comedy. With each successive film comedy he has been pulling out the stops more and more, and *The Great Race* (dedicated to Blake's boyhood idols, Mr. Laurel and Mr. Hardy) goes whole hog—even to a wild pie-throwing scene. With his wry sense of humor, Blake will say, "They may not like it, but they can't say it's like anything else." The same might be said of its creator. He's one of a kind.

Blake Edwards Talks about Budgets, Real and Exaggerated

Sue Cameron / 1971

From the *Hollywood Reporter*, 1971. Reprinted by permission of Sue Cameron.

"I think that my reputation in this industry is most unfair—I could just kill it makes me so mad. I started at Columbia Pictures making twelve-day musicals. Everything I have done, with three exceptions, has been on schedule and on, or under, budget—from the TV series *Peter Gunn* and *Mr. Lucky* to *Days of Wine and Roses*, *Breakfast at Tiffany's*, and *The Pink Panther*. Even *The Party* was on schedule and on budget."

So says Blake Edwards, angry at what he feels is an unjust reputation.

"This whole thing is a game," continued Edwards, "and one that the new guys at the studio learn fast. I learned from Harry Cohn. You learn you're going to be stolen from by distributors; departments are going to come in with padded budgets, so if by chance they spend less they can say to the big boss, 'Look, we saved you $1.98.' If you have a delinquent parent, you don't grow up well-adjusted. There's no morality where budgets are concerned; it's all one big studio game with the big pictures used as scapegoats."

The three exceptions to Edwards's record, he says, are *The Great Race*, *What Did You Do in the War, Daddy?* and *Darling Lili*.

"*The Great Race* was made for $12,000,000—at that time it was a lot of money. What the studio (Warners) won't say now is that to date it has grossed $22,000,000. On that picture I was lied to so much by the studio I walked off the set," he says.

On *Darling Lili*, Edwards says, "If I were to tell you everything that went on with Paramount, lawyers would get involved. I have been thinking of doing that anyway, but I don't want to discuss that aspect. I will say *Darling Lili* was budgeted at $11,000,000. It cost $16,700,000. I wanted to shoot the aerial sequences in the South and the studio wanted to use the Irish Air Force.

"They sent us over there without even checking the weather reports to see what Ireland was like. I kept trying to tell them that Ireland only has something like eighty-four sunny days a year. We lost thirty shooting days there at $50,000 a day. But the studio neglects to mention that they got $2,000,000 of it back in insurance.

"I knew all along things were being done to my production by different regimes of people, but it got to a point where it was virtually hopeless and I couldn't fight anymore. I didn't even get to see the ad campaign before it went out."

Edwards declines to discuss *What Did You Do in the War, Daddy?* except to say he believes the antiwar concept was ahead of its time, and he cautioned the studio against making the picture at all.

Edwards also talked about Julie Andrews, now his wife, who he feels is another victim of gossip.

"Julie did *Star* on an old 20th commitment," Edwards says. "Everyone was saying she got $1,000,000 cash plus 10 percent of the gross. That is absolutely not true. She got $200,000 flat and no percentage. Somebody had to be the goat for the studio's mistakes, and the star system was it. Julie worked harder on that picture than any other and all she got for it was unfair comments," Edwards says.

Another picture that upset Edwards and Miss Andrews was *Thoroughly Modern Millie*. Edwards says at this point that "Julie would never say these things that I'm saying because she is too much of a lady, but I think they should be told."

"Julie asked Universal to please just make *Millie* a little film. It would have been a classic that way, but, no, they wanted to capitalize on her popularity. They put back all the scenes that were cut to make it long enough for a roadshow. Julie was sick about it, but they ignored her.

"On her TV special with Harry Belafonte, everyone printed that she got $375,000 for doing it. What people don't know is that she gave all that away to build a Hathaway Home for children on the De Mille Ranch. But once again she didn't want people to know she gave the money away because she doesn't do things for publicity."

Edwards is currently making *The Wild Rovers* for MGM for $3,000,000. It stars William Holden, Ryan O'Neal, Tom Skerritt, James Olsen, and Joe Don Baker.

"It is a contemporary story in a classic setting," he says. "It is the story of a young and old cowboy and their exploits. It has a fairy-tale quality but also will hit home the point that people shouldn't be labeled or categorized. I really am enjoying making this movie. I feel that it is really special—and I think that it's time everyone bury the hatchet, and the whole industry get on with the business of making movies."

Blake Edwards Interview—In the Lair of the Pink Panther

Peter Stamelman / 1977

From *Millimeter*, January 1977, pp. 18–20, 22, 72–75. Reprinted by permission of Peter Stamelman.

The hallmarks of a Blake Edwards film are energy, drive, wit, visual elegance, and, above all, style. These qualities also apply to the man himself: he drives a spanking new Ferrari (still bearing its original Italian plates), sports sunglasses indoors and out, wears tailored French jeans and Adidas Superstars, and manages to transform, by his mere presence, his otherwise very drab, nondescript 20th Century-Fox offices into a villa on the Côte d'Azur. No wonder his films have style—the man himself reeks of it.

He has just finished directing his twenty-second film, *The Pink Panther Strikes Again*, which he also co-wrote with Frank Waldman. Edwards began his career as a writer-producer; he and a friend made *Panhandle* for Monogram on a miniscule budget. From there he worked in radio on the Richard Diamond series with Dick Powell, then wrote *Sound Off*, directed by Richard Quine, for Mickey Rooney. He wrote several more films for Quine, including such memorable comedies as *Operation Madball* (1957) and *The Notorious Landlady* (1962). His own directing career began in 1955 with *Bring Your Smile Along* starring Frankie Laine. He proceeded to direct five more B features for Columbia and Universal before he got his break: *Operation Petticoat* (1959) with Cary Grant and Tony Curtis and with a screenplay by Edwards and his long-time collaborator Maurice Richlin.

In 1961 he left the farm system and joined the majors for good with *Breakfast at Tiffany's*. He has batted close to or above .300 ever since with only three exceptions to his otherwise unbroken string of critical and commercial hits—and they are interesting exceptions at that—*The Great Race* (1965), *What Did You Do in the War, Daddy?* (1966), and *Darling Lili* (1969). Edwards is by now generally recognized as one of our first-rate directors or, more properly, screenwriter-directors.

(Andrew Sarris, in his book *The American Cinema*, positions Edwards amidst the august company of Capra, Cukor, Minnelli, Ray, et al., in his "Far Side of Paradise" category.) The films of Blake Edwards generate interest and respect the world over, and he is truly an international figure of the cinema.

But all has not been sweetness and light in either his career or his personal life. This was particularly true after *Darling Lili* in 1969 and again in 1972 at the time of *The Carey Treatment*'s release. On both occasions he was ready to quit the business, especially in '69 when he and his wife, Julie Andrews, were being examined, lectured, and second-guessed in the gossip columns and in studio boardrooms. Edwards made some trenchant, caustic, and on-target statements about Hollywood and filmmaking at that time, and I begin the interview by reading him one of those statements to see how he feels about it today.

Millimeter: You said in early 1970, at the time of all the problems with *Darling Lili*, "filmmaking is one of the rare businesses—and I still hate calling it a business—in which unqualified people sit in parasitical positions and destroy creative talent." Do you think that is still true today?

Blake Edwards: Yes, I do, very definitely. People who truly are not qualified to make creative judgments are constantly imposing their ignorance on creative people. Their cop-out is always the same: it is a business, and there are business "considerations." Okay, I'll grant them that—sure you've got to think of budgets and distribution; you've got to think of all of that. But as far as I'm concerned all of that means absolutely nothing if the creative judgment in the beginning is no good. If it is a business, then it means you're dealing with product, and if your product isn't any good, then the business suffers. Okay—who manufactures the product? They (studio executives) spend a lot of money to get creative people to manufacture the product, and then they invariably come up with the platitude, after you've finished the picture, "Well, you know, you're too close to it; therefore, you can't make the right decision." *Too close to it!* Incredible! (Edwards laughs heartily.) I become fascinated by their dying proclamations of movies being a business, and then they run it like a joke. Take this analogy: they are the board of directors of an oil company, and they go out and hire the world's best geologist to figure out where to drill. They spend a lot of money, and he goes out and figures out where to drill and comes back to tell them his findings. They say, "You've been working too hard. You're too close to the project. We shouldn't put it in there; we're going to put it in over there." That's the kind of madness that prevails in our business.

MM: Are you saying that the creative people are infallible?

BE: No, not at all. Of course we make mistakes. But you've got to start with the premise that if you're good enough to be hired in the first place, then you are the person who is better equipped to make fewer mistakes. Certainly the people who hired you could never replace you or do your [the director's] job in a million years. Now I suppose it has gotten a little better in the last few years. I know the best experiences that I've ever had have been on these last two *Pink Panther* films for United Artists. Eric Pleskow (president of U.A.) says to you right out in front, "You're the moviemaker; I'm the distributor. You have the expertise in one area; we have it in another. You will make the final creative judgments, but we'll make the final judgments in distribution. We'll both have input—we'll tell you what we feel about the films, but you don't have to accept it." And U.A. puts up hard, solid money! I must say it's refreshing, and it works very, very well. The interesting thing is that when a director gets that kind of freedom, when they say to you right out front, "Okay, we trust you; we'll go with you," it makes you a terribly responsible, loyal director. You really want to go out and do your best because they've shown you that kind of trust.

MM: After you completed *Operation Petticoat* in 1959 you said that working on that picture with Cary Grant had taught you some bitter, but valuable, lessons. I take it *Operation Petticoat* was one of your first experiences with creative problems.
BE: Simply put, there were enormous differences of opinion between Cary and myself. Being a new director who was getting his first chance at doing something that could turn out to be very important in his career, I was in a very ambivalent position. I did decide early on that I would stand by my guns and fight it through as best I could because I felt that if I compromised too much, I really would never know whether or not I could direct and control a picture. It ended up being a rather unpleasant experience because there *was* great personal conflict between Cary and myself. But I did prove to myself that if you believed in something, it was important to stand up for it—even if you found out later you were wrong. In the final analysis I wasn't intimidated by Cary's star presence, so even though I lost some of the battles on that picture, I also really learned a lot—about moviemaking and myself.

MM: Your next film, *Breakfast at Tiffany's* (1961), was the one that really brought Blake Edwards to the attention of many people. When you took the project, did you see it as a major turning point in your career?
BE: Oh, yes, definitely.

MM: The seven films that you had done prior to *Tiffany's*, were they the films you really wanted to do?
BE: No . . . well, yes, they were. Look, what the hell, when you're starting out as a director . . . just to be able to direct, particularly at that time (the mid-fifties) when

there wasn't as rebellious a feeling out here, when youth wasn't being considered as much as today, when you were really fighting the system even more than today. At that time it was a thrill for me just to get the opportunity. But I knew those films were just a beginning step. Because there were still B films in those days and that was basically what I was directing before *Tiffany's*. You knew those films would be released in a particular way, that they would be mildly received by the second-string critics . . . the expectations weren't as great as when you did an A picture. Young directors today don't have that chance—when I started out you had more of a chance to fail but still bounce back. You had a training camp. Today *every* picture is the big one, they're all A pictures.

MM: What particularly attracted you to *Breakfast at Tiffany's*?

BE: First and foremost the chance to work with Audrey Hepburn. That to me was an indication that people believed in me. Of course, I also like the book, though I must tell you, were I offered the project today, I would insist on being more faithful to the Holly Golightly that Capote really wrote about. At that time we couldn't have gotten away with it. But that was the story I wanted to make, and, quite frankly, I don't know if Audrey would have wanted to play *that* Holly.

MM: You seem to have a knack for casting character roles with fresh, memorable faces. Is that something you deliberately set out to do?

BE: Sure, I try to do that. What I like to do is cast against type. When I was looking for the actor to play Peter Gunn, for instance, I took my cue from Dick Powell in *Murder My Sweet*: his whole career had gone downhill, he was an ex-musical comedy star singing by a waterfall—then suddenly here he was playing a private eye and doing it most effectively. I applied that same principle to Craig Stevens, who had been a Warners' B-leading man, and I took him to the Westmores, had his hair cut off, gave him a new wardrobe, and suddenly that casting against type really worked for me. Craig *was* my Peter Gunn.

MM: After *Tiffany's* you did a complete about-face and directed your first thriller [and ~~your~~ first film in black and white] *Experiment in Terror* (1962). Were you testing yourself, trying new challenges?

BE: Sure. I think that period of my life was a constant testing; I really didn't know where I was going. I remember one critic saying, "We don't know who or what Blake Edwards is." Well, I didn't know either! I wanted to constantly explore and if I found whatever it was I wanted most, then I would pursue that. But, you know, I'm *still* exploring; I don't think I have ever really found out "who or what Blake Edwards is." I just can't be labelled and that is a helluva lot more stimulating for me.

MM: Why have you returned to the *Pink Panther* films? Your latest, *The Pink Panther Strikes Again*, will be your fourth in the series.

BE: For a very simple reason: I am a realist, a practical man. I like to make films, and in order for me to continue making films, I've got to get somebody to put up the money. My decision to do *The Return of the Pink Panther* two years ago was a very calculating move on my part. I always seem to be able to guess trends, and I truly believed that the public was ready and primed for another *Pink Panther* film. Granted I must also admit that I was certainly aware of how important merchandising had become and the enormous success of the cartoons; that input just served to strengthen my judgment that the time was right. Also, quite frankly, my career was at a bit of a low and I needed a hit.

MM: You directed the first *Pink Panther* in 1964. How did the whole thing begin?

BE: It was craziness: an old friend of mine, Maurice Richlin, came to see me. I was under contract to the Mirisch brothers at the time. Maurice had an idea about a jewel theft. I wasn't particularly interested in the jewel theft itself, but I began to become interested in the very involved relationships: a police inspector who was so blind to everything but his job that he didn't realize that his wife was stocking up on mink coats and that she was actually the mistress of one of the world's greatest jewel thieves—in fact, the very man the inspector was hunting. It was also a wonderful kind of put-on of the whole Cary Grant–*To Catch a Thief* syndrome.

MM: Did you envision Clouseau as a kind of bumbling, comic counterpoint to James Bond?

BE: Yes, sure, that was there, too. I love to debunk myths, to be iconoclastic. I like my policemen to be fallible; even though they don't like it, I prefer that all my policemen be as fallible as you or I. The beauty that hooked me on Clouseau is that he really represents us all. I've said this before, but it's worth repeating: Clouseau's 11th commandment is "Thou shalt not give up." He is really a very noble character, in spite of everything, in spite of himself. I think that's a wonderful message to give to people.

MM: In that same year, 1964, you also did *A Shot in the Dark*, with Sellers again playing Clouseau. You were actually called in on short notice to replace Anatole Litvak, and the film was originally going to star Sophia Loren and Walter Matthau. What is the story behind all this?

BE: It was a fluke. Sellers, who was scheduled to be in it along with Loren and Matthau, didn't like the script, and he told the Mirisch brothers that he wasn't going to do it. In desperation Harold Mirisch called me because apparently Sellers did say he would do it only if I directed it. I read the script and told Harold that I would consider doing it if I was allowed to make some major changes, including changing the character that Sellers was supposed to play into somebody that better suited him: Inspector Clouseau. The film had an impossible schedule—we were supposed to go on the stages in eight weeks. So U.A. and the Mirisch brothers said go ahead, and I said, "You must give me carte blanche on this one, fellas, because I'm not sure exactly what I'm going to do." They agreed, and I flew to New York. On the way I worked out a plot-line. In New York I met with the production manager and art director who had flown in from England. I gave them just a step outline of what I was going to need; I didn't really know yet what I was going to shoot. They flew back to England to start constructing, and I got on a boat with William Peter Blatty. We wrote half the screenplay going across the Atlantic. Four weeks later we had a completed screenplay, and we were cast because I was casting as we were writing. Sophia found out that the script was being changed and why, so we lost her. Matthau also dropped out after the script changes. But eight weeks later we were on that stage and shooting. It was incredible!

MM: Your next film *The Great Race* (1964) received some pretty bad notices. Did the film do well at the box office?
BE: It was successful, though certainly not as successful as I would have liked it to have been.

MM: Did you intend *The Great Race* to be almost the definitive slapstick comedy?
BE: Well, that sounds a bit presumptuous; let's just say I wanted to break new ground. I wanted to try some new things.

MM: Weren't you going to direct *The Planet of the Apes*?
BE: Yes, I was, but a couple of things happened. First of all, Warners and I were having a big battle about *The Great Race*. Second, the approach by Arthur Jacobs (*Planet*'s producer) to the project had changed so much that I decided I didn't want to be involved. Put simply, Arthur wanted a money-maker, which was okay, but I also felt that the film really had something to say.

MM: You had two other projects at that time that sounded interesting but that never got off the ground: *Gettysburg* and a project with Jack Lemmon called *The Toy Soldier*. What happened?
BE: Well, with *Gettysburg*, the immense size of the project just scared everybody off. It was a monumentally important film and could not be done cheaply. *The Toy Soldier* just went the way of many projects in this town, even though we had Jack and he was hot to do it. It just fell apart, and I don't know exactly why.

MM: Your next film, after *The Great Race*, was *What Did You Do in the War, Daddy?* (1966). The film was not a success, either critically or financially, though it does seem to have a strong cult following.

BE: Do you know that is my wife's favorite Blake Edwards film? I don't want to sound like an I-told-you-so fella, but again it was a matter of typecasting. I wanted to do *Toy Soldier* and Walter Mirisch, to whom I was under contract, wanted me to do *War/Daddy* because he felt I was a comedy director and he didn't want me to get involved in anything heavy. I told him that I didn't think it was a good time to do a war comedy—it was right in the middle of the Vietnam War. There were a lot of Gold Star mothers, and the perspective on war was not what it should be for this kind of satire. Also I myself was having serious domestic, personal problems—my marriage was heading for the rocks, and I was about to get a divorce. I told Mirisch that I couldn't leave the country because I didn't want to leave my kids behind. So it meant that I would have to do *War/Daddy* here, and it wouldn't have the documentary look that it needed. In order for the film to work it had to look real, and that meant shooting in Italy. Instead we built the whole goddamn village out in Chatsworth or Thousand Oaks. And instead of using real Italians we used American "Italians." So there really was much that didn't work. Despite all that, however, I must say I still love the film. I watch it occasionally, and I still get lots of laughs. It was a black comedy way ahead of its time.

MM: *The Party*, in 1968, marked your ninth film with a score by Henry Mancini. He has also scored most of your films since then. It is rare to find such a long, almost unbroken collaboration between director and composer. How and when did your association begin?

BE: In '57, I was doing a film for Universal called *Mr. Cory*. I felt that the film needed a romantic theme song; Hank was working at Universal at that time, and they brought me some of his music. It was very pretty, and I thought, "Somebody is one helluva melody writer around here." I was introduced to him. Dissolve. Three years later I was getting ready to do *Peter Gunn*, and I bumped into Hank in the commissary and asked him if he'd like to do a television show. He said sure as long as he could use jazz. I told him, "Sure, you can do anything you want." That began a beautiful relationship; I mean, the minute I heard what he had written for *Peter Gunn* I knew I had found a winner. We segued on to *Mr. Lucky*, and then I began using him for my films. You see, I love melody, and Hank is one of the great exponents of true melody. He's from the Victor Young school. I love his sense of humor; Hank has one of the greatest senses of humor in the whole world. And another thing: he has never been wrong about any of my films. He is the most accurate barometer. . . . I listen to Hank because he's spontaneous, very uncomplicated . . .

he just goes! The things he says are almost always right, so in addition to being a great composer he's a great critic.

MM: *Darling Lili* (1969) seems to have been an ill-fated project right from the beginning . . .

BE: Oh, that was such a bad experience for me. It was particularly bad because Julie Andrews and I were an item for the first time. It's fascinating what other factors came into play aside from the film itself. The fact that Julie and I were in love and living together . . . I guess everybody felt Mary Poppins was getting soiled or something. It's funny: as much as I know about this town, about just how cruel and tasteless it can be, I still find that I'm terribly naive. I'm positive that all those extraneous elements hurt *Darling Lili*. Now beyond all that were the terrible problems I had with Paramount and that whole hierarchy. They interfered and even got involved on a personal, vindictive level. It is still hard to talk about it now; it was that painful. There is documented evidence—letters, memos—that I sent from Europe saying, "Get me home; you're going to lose control of this financially. Get it on a soundstage." Eventually they did, but much too late. The fact that they sent me to Ireland when my thirteen-year-old daughter knows, for Chrissakes, how rotten the weather is there, especially for a movie like *Darling Lili*. I had wanted to go to South Carolina, where they had a number of German World War I planes, but Paramount wanted Ireland because they had all those planes from *The Blue Max* there. One thing began to compound another: Charlie Bluhdorn and Gulf & Western had taken over. Now, I had already had a major run-in with Bluhdorn when I was doing the film version of *Peter Gunn* (1967). He had sent me a cable telling me to put a certain actress in the role of Edie, Pete's girl. It wasn't "I'd like to make a suggestion"; it was "I run the studio now and this is what I want." And I thought, "Be careful; anybody that is acting that powerful doesn't understand the business." So I ran a screen test on the girl, and she was German! She could barely speak English! It was insane—I sent a wire back telling him that my contract stipulated such and such, etc. etc. . . . So Bluhdorn didn't like me from the start. The things that happened on *Darling Lili* . . . someday I'll have to tell the whole story.

MM: It was sadly ironic that right after that you locked horns (as did many others) with James Aubrey at MGM; it involved *The Wild Rovers* (1971).

BE: That's when I first started thinking about quitting. It was my best film, and he butchered it. I begged, I pleaded, I beseeched them, and they still butchered it. So I said, "Fuck 'em!" But then I did a foolish thing: I allowed myself to be coerced or seduced or whatever. Aubrey got me in, and he even apologized [for his handling of *The Wild Rovers*]. He said, "But here's a project—*The Carey Treatment*—that I know you're right for, and we'll stay out of it." He was lying through his teeth—he was actually out to crucify me. The things that happened back in Boston [where *Carey* was shot] . . .

MM: I want to get back to *The Wild Rovers*: is there a complete print anywhere?
BE: (with a kind of weary resignation) No, I don't even have one myself. A year and a half ago when I hit with *Return of the Pink Panther* and everybody was suddenly my friend again, I went to the new regime at Metro to see if an original print was still available. I said to them, "Please let me release it in one theater; let people see what the original film was. *Please!* I'll pay for it; I'll four-wall it; I'll do the whole thing." This spread around Metro, and the next report I got was that the film had been destroyed. The only people who saw the original print were Arthur Knight and his cinema class at USC. They loved it; Arthur felt it was my best film . . .

MM: I take it *The Carey Treatment* (1972) also got the "Aubrey treatment."
BE: Yeah, it sure did. As I've said, I was making so much heat about what he'd done to *Rovers* that he called me in and gave me *Carey* as a "consolation." He knew full well he was going to destroy it. It was after that that I really quit. I left the business, went to Switzerland to live. I told Julie, "That's it—I'm through with this." I had such good things planned for *Carey* . . .

MM: But you did, obviously, come back to directing. You did *The Tamarind Seed* (1974) for Lew Grade and ITC. It did quite well at the box office despite lukewarm critical reaction. It cost $2.4 million to make, yet looks like a $5 or $6 million film. Was this your way of answering the Bluhdorns and Aubreys and others who said you couldn't bring a film in on time and on budget?
BE: Not really. I have long since given up trying to prove anything to those guys—or to anybody else. I spent my entire career bringing films in under budget. *Darling Lili,* because of all the publicity, gave everybody the wrong impression; the lies and distortions that Paramount came out with snow-jobbed everybody, even those who should know better. For example, about a month ago I watched Charles Champlin interview Robert Evans on television. Now Charles Champlin is a reputable gentleman; he *usually* knows his facts. And he said that he had heard that the cost of *Darling Lili* was $26 million or some equally outrageous figure. Evans, to his everlasting discredit, didn't correct him! Instead he said something like, "Well, no, it wasn't quite that much." He knew goddamn well that the actual cost was nowhere near that. He was in a position to set the record straight, and he didn't. Not only that but then he [Evans] said that the film never made its advertising costs back, which is a bloody, direct lie! Paramount went out and made a deal with Commonwealth-United and laid the whole picture off. The whole thing—and I hate like hell to say it because it sounds so damned paranoiac—but the whole

thing is a conspiracy. Bluhdorn was even quoted as making a statement in the South of France that he was going to get me; he did everything he could to do just that.

I did *Tamarind* on a very low budget and then did *Return of the Pink Panther* for a little over $2 million, which, by today's standards, is low, especially considering the production values I got in those two pictures. But still that *Darling Lili* reputation haunts me. After I finished *Return of the Pink Panther* I'm sitting in a studio executive's office, and he says to me, "Yeah, but when you go over budget, you *really* go over budget." So I said, "Based on what, for Chrissakes?" and he says, "*Darling Lili*." Now I'm steaming: "Yeah, do you know what the budget *was* on *Darling Lili?*" "Well, I heard . . ." "Yeah, but do you *really* know?" "Well, no. . ." "Now, what other pictures have I ever gone over budget on?" "None." That's right! I got my training at Columbia—Harry Cohn would have fired my ass if I went one penny over.

It's nothing to bring a picture in on schedule or under budget. The hard part is making a good picture—I don't care what your schedule or budget is. My best defense is my pictures themselves; they speak for themselves. They tell the story.

Advertisement from Eastman Kodak Company

The Hollywood Reporter / 1979

From *The Hollywood Reporter,* February 28, 1979. Reprinted by permission of the Eastman Kodak Company.

Blake Edwards, writer-director-producer and father of the irrepressible Pink Panther, talks about comedy, directing, film, and making it in the business he loves so well.

"I think great comedy is based on human frailty—avarice, greed. In Clouseau's case, it deals with a very human characteristic that the late Gene Fowler called the 11th Commandment: 'Thou shalt not give up.'

"After the first Panther, we began to investigate Clouseau more. We talked on many occasions about who his tailor is—that terrible man who sells him those awful clothes. And why does he have a manservant who puts up with the things that man puts up with? These things will never be known by the audience, but they are sort of the underpinning of the character.

"Movies have become a director's medium. Maybe a better word than director would be *filmmaker*. But by whatever name, he has the final say—on the script, the acting, the edit, and the performances—everything. And if the movie is a failure, it's his failure. So he takes a lot on himself.

"An interesting thing happens to me on the set—I really cannot remember lines I have written. A producer once said about me that as a director I could say, 'Who the heck wrote that?' and then turn around later as the writer and say, 'Who the heck directed that scene of mine?'

"I've always used Kodak film. They keep coming up with the kind of film that makes my job that much easier. For example, I used to hate to shoot day for night. Somehow you always see a brute or a light shining, and you can't just buy it. Soon I'll be shooting in Mexico near a lot of structures that are gleaming white, white, white. With a full moon we'll be able to shoot that for real. We'll be able to say, 'That looks *real*—there's the reflection off the sea, so there's depth. Terrific!' Because then it becomes more real. For me, the more real the picture, the more believable the action.

"Making it as a newcomer takes determination. Humility is not one of the prerequisites. The very nature of what you are doing is show-offish. You are God-like. You are on the set directing and you are *it*. It's very egocentric.

"I would say to young filmmakers, let's see that fire burning under there. Be a little opinionated and a little I-know-more-than-anybody-else. And then I'd say, with all those qualities—cool it. Because in today's terms it is better to be cool about your attitudes in front of people. Remember, nothing is new—no matter how good we are, it has all been done before."

S.O.B.: Blake Edwards's Blast at His Real-Life Blacklisting

Rena Le Blanc / 1979

From *Los Angeles* magazine, vol. 24, no. 5, May 1979, pp. 292–93. Reprinted by permission of Rena Dictor Le Blanc.

To hear Blake Edwards tell it, the reasons why he and wife Julie Andrews have only recently returned to Hollywood after six years in exile are the stuff of which soap operas are made. Despite a strong track record as a producer, director, and writer on such hits as *The Pink Panther*, *Experiment in Terror*, *The Notorious Landlady*, *Days of Wine and Roses*, and *A Shot in the Dark*, Edwards found himself an outcast because of one flop—an expensive disaster called *Darling Lili*, which made him a number of powerful enemies and, he claims, "nearly broke my psychic back."

Much of that injury has healed now, and Edwards is making his comeback—in the town that rejected him—by directing *10*, a comedy that stars his wife and Dudley Moore. More importantly, he's also gearing up to produce a screenplay inspired by the events that drove him into exile. Called *S.O.B.*, the film will be a roman à clef exposing the behind-the-scenes maneuvers of some highly recognizable Hollywood power mongers. Some might call it revenge; Edwards prefers to think of it as a catharsis.

"I just drew on my knowledge of the film business in writing the movie," Edwards explains. In *S.O.B.* a highly successful producer has just endured a gigantic film failure, and his life takes on an air of zany doom. His wife takes off with the kids; there are bloodletting reviews of his movie. There's an inept suicide attempt, pornography, madness, body snatching, and even a Viking burial at sea.

According to Edwards, "What happens to Felix [the film's main character] is symbolic of what happens to a lot of people who have their creativity usurped by people in charge of studios who are making creative decisions they didn't have the credentials to make.

"The script is full of people you know," he continues. "There's an agent, for instance. You can't miss her. She's a man-eater, a shark.

"Julie will star in the film, and she'll bare her breasts for the first time. And she says she'll get a kick out of doing it."

S.O.B. was born following a period in which, as Edwards puts it, "I was really in a lot of pain. After my last experience I said, 'Well, that's it. I'm not going to direct anymore. I'm going to get out of town. Either I'm not emotionally strong enough to handle it, or it's too heavy for anybody under these conditions.'"

Edwards's troubles began when Paramount decided to film *Darling Lili* in Ireland despite his warnings about weather problems. The first day of shooting a complex battle scene was a success. But by the second day the weather had changed, and the cameras stopped rolling because the film had to have the same weather.

"The second day, Charles Bluhdorn [head of Gulf and Western, which had just acquired Paramount] showed up with his wife and could not comprehend why we weren't filming. I sat him down and explained it to him. He never did accept the explanation.

"He finally left the location in an outrage. He took a cap with DARLING LILI printed on it and threw it across the room. He said, 'That S.O.B. Blake Edwards, I'll crucify him for spending my money,' or words to that effect.

"Eventually," Edwards recalls, "the situation got to be like *Gaslight*"—the classic film where Charles Boyer plots to drive Ingrid Bergman crazy. "They would say things to me and deny saying them, or not say things to me and claim they had said them. I became so paranoid that I was writing letters saying, 'For God's sake, get us out of here.'" And to make things even worse, Edwards claims Bluhdorn told him, "If the film's not a success, you're dead. You're hung." Bluhdorn was unavailable for comment about Edwards's charges.

Edwards insists that it's unheard of to threaten a director in such a manner—especially before he finishes his film. "I mean, the lies, the deceit that went on. I finally was so whipped. My self-esteem was at such a low ebb. I was just torn to pieces."

Finally, Edwards says, he confronted Bob Evans, then the head of the studio, in his office in Hollywood: "I said, 'You've lied to me. You have demeaned me and my wife. A hundred years ago at least I would have had the prerogative of slapping you across the face with a glove, and we'd have gone out and settled it man to man. At least give me that much. Step outside. I've just got to get this out of my system.'"

Instead, he says, Evans retreated behind his desk, lit a cigar, and ordered Edwards thrown out. Thinking back on the incident, Edwards says with a grin, "I've never done that before or since in the film business."

Evans, however, denies he ever lied to or deceived Edwards. And Evans recalls neither Edwards's challenge to fight him nor his order to have the director thrown out of his office. "I think these are all figments of his imagination," says Evans, who currently is a producer at Paramount.

"I worked very collaboratively with him on the picture," Evans claims. "I protected him. I always believed in the film. I was wrong. He was going so far over budget in the picture and spending money so capriciously that I had to look into it. The picture was the biggest financial fiasco the company's ever had."

Edwards contends the film was a disaster because the people with the money kept exercising creative control. He warned them the film had too many musical numbers, too much plane fighting. But he maintains the money people responded, "Well, we spent all this money, so the footage stays in."

Budgeted for about $11 million, the film costs hit $16 million according to Edwards—and $20 million according to Evans. Says Edwards, "They laid it at my feet and said it was my inability to keep controls.

"This was not the first time I made a failure," he says. "I just never made one on this kind of grand scale. I was really persona non grata for a while."

He had already contracted for another film at a different studio, however, and he proceeded with it. "It started all over again," he recalls. "I found out I was dealing with a man who had no honor, was very destructive, and had absolutely no conscience. He would, for expedience sake, tell you anything and the next day say, 'Well, sue me.'"

Once, the producer offered Edwards's fifteen-year-old daughter some cocaine. Edwards hit the ceiling, yelling in front of the entire crew, "If you get near her again, I'll kill you or get somebody to do it."

Later, Edwards was approached by a hit man, who offered to follow through on the threat. "That's how bizarre, how sick it was," he says. "That's no more extreme than a dozen other things that were happening. I thought that if it's deteriorated to that degree, I've got to get out."

The events so shattered Edwards that he backed off completely from the film scene in order to "lick my wounds," taking his wife and children first to London and later to rural Switzerland, where he and Andrews switched roles completely. While she was the breadwinner, he stayed home and cared for the children and household. "I was really the mother," Edwards explains. "She'd come staggering home and say, 'Guess what happened at work?' and I would say, 'Let me tell you about the kids.' She was a tower of strength for me. She was a person who wouldn't consider letting me run away from it completely." When his wounds from Hollywood had begun to heal a bit, Andrews started telling her husband that the time had come for him to get on with his career.

Recuperating gradually, Edwards went back to work in Europe, producing *The Pink Panther Strikes Again* and *Revenge of the Pink Panther* between 1976 and 1978. And he began pondering the Hollywood scene from a distance. "Little by little I began to see the insanity of it," he recalls. "And I thought, as I have many times in the past, 'I've got to write about it. I'll get my demons out of the way.'" The result was the script for S.O.B.

Despite the tragic overtones, Edwards intends S.O.B. to be a comedy. "Julie says it's the best thing I've ever written," he boasts. "But it's been turned down on every front." Given the habit that film execs have of protecting each other, it's likely that no major studio will back the film. But Edwards has an answer for that, too. If he can't get a studio to cooperate, he'll simply finance the film himself.

Seminar with Blake Edwards

American Film Institute / 1979

From AFI's Harold Lloyd Master Seminar © 1979, courtesy of American Film Institute. Reprinted by permission.

[Ed. Note: Interview takes place after a screening of Edwards's not-yet-released new film 10.]

Interviewer (James Powers): I'm very pleased to introduce to you Blake Edwards. The film you've just seen is called 10. I guess it's more or less finished except for—

BE: Dubbing and scoring.

JP: When I had originally asked Blake, I thought we'd show the *Pink Panther* movies and talk about comedy, and then he generously offered to show this film. Would you like to share some of your feelings about it? Or if any of you have questions about this film, we can start from there.

Question: I don't get to see a picture in its unfinished form that often, and I was wondering how you're affected by audience response before the picture is actually locked. I realize there's still effects to be laid in.

BE: I'm affected a lot. I show the hell out of a film, usually with an audience about like this. I show it to close personal friends, and I take into account they're close personal friends; I pay attention to what they're saying. And I show it to a group of total strangers—a varied audience. Usually with out-and-out comedy, I'll also preview it many times, so that I have a bigger audience to react to. This one, I'm not taking it out to preview because I just don't think it needs it. I mean, I know what works and what doesn't. I know it very well at this point.

Question: Insomuch as the sound, I don't know what exactly is missing, both music and effects.

BE: Music and effects are missing, yes.

Question: Can you bolster comedy? Can you put it—we're not talking about laughter, but I'm saying can you really punctuate something to actually elicit a laugh?

BE: I think you can help a laugh by—I can't be specific because I can't think of anything specific, but generally I think that something that's funny might be helped moderately with effects or music or something like that. The laugh is there or it isn't, and . . . I don't know. That's interesting. I can't think of any cases where I bolstered it or helped it with effects. I know it can be helped with effects if they're not there, and the idea of George in the boat is the first thing that comes to me. We got a dumb water track in there, score and wind and balance of voice and things like that will make it a lot better. It won't be funny; it'll be somewhat amusing that he's out in the boat. And if Hank [Mancini] scores it with very courageous music, that will help the total picture.

Question: So what I'm getting at is the comedy relies mostly on a visual form.

BE: I think so, yes. But you know, in moderate ways—for example, George running across the sand in certain areas, you don't hear him go (makes panting noise). Well, when those things are in, that'll make it *that* much funnier. When he first hits the sand way off in the distance, you'll hear him respond to it, so it'll help it that much. But if he isn't funny or if *it* isn't funny, there's not much you can do, in my opinion, with the sound or music that's going to make it funny.

Question: How much different is this version from the original George Segal *10*?

BE: Well, it's very much the same except that—well, obviously we refer to Dudley's size, have fun with it when he says, you know, I can't even ask him outside. And a lot of the way of speaking because Dudley's essentially English, the lines were pretty much the same, but they would be changed according to what was comfortable to Dudley. And Dudley is a wonderful physical comedian; he really is terrific—one of the best I've ever worked with. So we found things for him to do—ways of things for him to do, let's say, that would suit him, and I'm sure that George would have done it his way.

Question: Was the character always a composer?

BE: Yeah, yeah, it was always that. That's essentially true. We got very lucky in that Dudley is such a consummate musician, but it didn't change that much.

Question: Who wrote the screenplay?

BE: I did.

Question: It's an original?

BE: Yes.

Question: I'm wondering about a lot of the subplots that were woven in and out—the lyricist and the woman he meets at the resort. Even the husband and wife seemed to be a subplot of the main text.

BE: Why the subplots?

Question: Yes, and the priest who was more or less just used as a gag and then he left.

BE: Well, he wasn't used as a gag. He was there for a very specific reason. Every one of those people subplots led him to the girl. The priest said, "Yes, I just married this girl, and her father's a dentist"—which led him to the dentist, which led him to Mexico. So that they were all his means of finding his way to Mexico. That's the only answer I have. Okay? What else?

Question: I have read that at first, you never were going to do another *Pink Panther.*

BE: Yes.

Question: Then you turned around and said you were going to do another one, so you're not going to do it?

BE: No.

Question: But it said Peter Sellers was going to do another one.

BE: Yes. I've just given them permission to go ahead and do it because I am part owner in it. They couldn't do it without me, and they paid me a lot of money. (laughs)

Question: Is there a difference in the way you approach writing a dramatic scene versus a comedic scene?

BE: No.

Question: Or are you just—

BE: No, I just try to be as honest as I know how about it. This story is rooted in a lot of reality. I lived in the house on the hill. I had a telescope; there was a neighbor with a telescope. I was between marriages. The idea of the film came to me when I was on location in Brussels, and I was riding to work. I got a signal, I stopped, and there was a big Mercedes Benz that pulled up next to me. There was a bride in the back, and you couldn't see her because of all the lace and everything. And just for a split second, I fantasized: what if this was the most beautiful woman that I'd ever seen and fell in love, and she's off to get married? What do you do about something like that? Fortunately, she was ghastly. (laughs) But that stuck with me, and I used that. And middle age, all of that for me is very real. The songwriters I know. The man who wrote the song, as a matter of fact, is sitting in the audience tonight, one of my oldest and dearest friends, and I was brought up around that. I'm a product of that era. Most of it is rooted in fact. So when I approach writing something like that, I just—it's hard to know where it comes from. You get your essential story, and then you just go at it and try to be as honest with it as you can.

Question: From the director's standpoint, how much time do you spend with your actors before your shoot or on a set preparing a scene?
BE: Depends on what my schedule is. We made this—

Question: Ideally what do you do?
BE: We made this one fairly fast. I spend a lot of time rehearsing, a lot of time finding out what's best and how to do it. And I don't shoot much film. I never have. It's mostly done in rehearsal. If I sense that the spontaneity is going, then I usually roll a camera for better or for worse. I work—I have worked for a number of years with instant replay, a television, so that I can look at the choreography and see how it goes and check it out for myself.

Question: Who photographed 10?
BE: Frank Stanley.

Question: Did he work with the videotape playback system before?
BE: Yes. He had worked with me before. I've used it for a long time, so he was very familiar with it.

Question: Do you use it solely to check the performances, or do you also use it to—
BE: I use it as an overall, all-around tool. It's great for your script person because he or she can't miss. I mean, if they forget something and they want to check something, it makes an honest man of your operators. (laughs) There's no way he can screw you around because like Billy [unclear] was here, my operator was here because you immediately look at it and see if that's it. I think it's very valuable. A lot of directors don't use it—won't use it, just absolutely won't. They are in horror. They feel that it's going to somehow, I don't know, inhibit their creativity or something. But they're the boss, they can use it any way they want to. And it pays for itself.

Question: Do the actors watch the playback?
BE: Yes, usually. They usually do. I've never run into an actor who misuses it, ever,

including Mr. Sellers, who is very undecided about things and given to want to do them over and over again. But it's instant rushes is what it is. What the hell, it's the difference between going and seeing rushes tomorrow and seeing them now. You can keep the film and the tape, and if you want to go back and check a set-up, if you want to go back and see what your lighting was like, anything like that, there it is for you.

Question: Do you feel comfortable with actors seeing the rushes?
BE: I feel comfortable with actors seeing the rushes if they feel comfortable. If I spot very quickly that it's hurting their performance or making them insecure or they're not able to be objective about what they're doing or, in fact, if they're not able to be objective and it becomes a destructive thing, then I ask them not to see rushes. But I haven't run into that much; I really haven't.

Question: I've heard that you did a lot of improvisation with Sellers in the *Panther* movies, and then you just mentioned before that you like to rehearse a lot. Is that exploration and just indigenous to working with Sellers, or did you do that occasionally to—
BE: Depends on what kind of an actor I've got. If you work with Cary Grant, very little improv. I mean, he does Cary Grant and does it better than anybody, but there's not much room for that. But Peter is that kind of a person, particularly when you're dealing with that kind of comedy, and you begin to see things happen along the way. Of course, it isn't really truly improv. It starts out being that, but it becomes something that's very fixed after a while.

Question: But it grows as you rehearse it on the set?
BE: That's right. Yeah. Yeah.

Question: Do you find the set, when you're working like that, changes the way you'll attempt to block the scene in terms of the order that you might want to shoot and the choices of lenses? I mean the choices of master or close medium that you might want?
BE: I don't ever think about the camera in the beginning. I don't even bother with the camera. The first thing I do is get my people used to what they're doing and see where they're the most comfortable on the set and where they move. All of my sets are four walls so that I'm not stuck with having to avoid that one wall that's out or something like that. Once I block it and it's done, then I begin looking for my angles and see where it's best to shoot it from. So, the improv, all of that goes to finally building the scene until it's known; everybody is fixed and marked pretty much, and then we get the camera out. Sometimes that changes too when you

find out, well, for some reason maybe, something doesn't work with the camera, and you might shift it around a little bit. Frank Stanley, who is my operator from a long time ago, is one of the cameramen that over-lights everything. He'll go in and he'll just over-light the set. I mean, everything is lit is what I'm trying to say. Just general lighting so that when we finally get it set, it really is a very short time while he's putting in keys and things like that, which is a nice way to work. It doesn't take a hell of a long time, and it looks pretty nice.

Question: Somehow there's a very different kind of pacing that works very well in this, with respect to passages between the very muscular kind of humor. Is there any style or precedence in other movies for that kind of pacing or that kind of a style?

BE: I don't know. It's a dangerous one because you're walking a very fine line. And you just hope that it works. I see no reason why broad comedy can't work in deep drama, you know, because my life is full of it constantly—unexpected things. Right in the middle of the most serious thing, you're suddenly on a tangent over somewhere else and ridiculous things occur. I think that's what life is all about. So if you're lucky, it works. If people can identify with it, it works. You do stop things to look at something else and to laugh at it or to cry at it that may not even be relevant to what the core of your quest is. Yet it's, you know, the tapestry upon which you do your painting, or it's the background to it. And it hopefully can have a lot of flavors.

Question: Blake, is the title tentative?
BE: 10? No, that's it.

Question: You and Dudley Moore have such a marvelous combination. Have you thought of doing your next project with him?
BE: Yes, I am doing my next project with him.

Question: Will it be a similar film?
BE: Pardon?

Question: Similar?
BE: No, no. This is—well, it's a strange kind of comedy. It's a comedy called *The Ferret*, and it's kind of a combination hopefully of Hitchcock suspense and wild broad comedy within a kind of Harold Lloyd kind of comedy that comes out of the adventure more than the character, although the character is inept in this present situation which is always good for comedy. He's a joy to work with. He's terrific.

Question: I think my favorite scene was the scene where the lady served the tea. (laughs) How do you write a scene like that?
BE: You just do. I don't know. It came to me.

Question: Where did you find this marvelous person?
BE: I don't know. I really don't. She's just a figment of—I really don't know. As I wrote the minister, because when I first got the idea I thought obviously this minister's got to be a songwriter, you know? He has to do that. And then it began to grow, took a kind of shape of its own. Crazy lady.

Question: That's the kind of underlining or something, almost a kind of a throw-away that's characteristic of your style of comedy. The scene would have worked without it. You would have gotten the essence of what you wanted out of the scene, but that was just a wonderful thought. Do you consciously keep yourself aware of those things?
BE: Yes, that's the way I think. It's essentially me. Those kinds of things I, for some reason, see all the time. I'm looking for kind of the crazy side, the black side. You know, without trying to sound deeply psychoanalytical, it's the thing that's gotten me through my life. I think I probably would have at one time or another jumped off a building if I hadn't been able to resort to that kind of madness, that kind of humor—to turn my madness into that, into laughing. The absurdity of life and not take it quite so seriously.

Question: Yes. I'd like to say that I enjoyed the picture, and I thought the editing was wonderful. I'd like to know a little bit more about that.
BE: Why don't you ask this gentleman right back there? There's the editor, Mr. Ralph Winters.

Question: How long did you have to cut the picture?
Ralph Winters: What was the question?

Question: How long did you have to cut the picture?
BE: About an hour and a half. (laughs)
RW: No specific time.

Question: Were you on location with the director?
RW: No, not on this one.

Question: And were there some difficult areas that didn't cut together well, or were there some particular problems there to overcome?

BE: You can tell the truth, Ralph.

RW: Well, there's always some problems. (laughs) You try to hide them.

Question: Yeah. Well, it was beautifully done. I was curious if you really adhered to the script.

RW: We never have any time-problems cutting pictures with Blake because he never asks when he can see something. He always says, "When you get it ready to look at . . ." Big difference.

BE: You have to remember too that Ralph and I have worked together since *Shot in the Dark*, wasn't it? Was that the first, Ralph?

RW: *The Pink Panther.*

BE: Yes, that's right, *Pink Panther*, the first *Pink Panther*.

Question: Well, I thought it had very good pacing, and I liked it a lot. There were a lot of—

BE: Thank you.

Question: Very charming scenes.

BE: Thank you.

Question: What do the people at UA think about the title?

BE: This is not a UA picture. No, no, Orion. What do they think about it? I don't know. I have not heard that they didn't like it. I think—why?

Question: I think it would be a hard name to market because it's not very descriptive.

BE: Well, I think it depends. I think it depends on the copy that goes along with 10, whether or not—what is the thing that they're using?

[inaudible]

BE: Yes, but something before that, something—

JP: A sophisticated comedy for adults.

BE: Not sophisticated. There's a couple of good words for adults who can count. . . . Yeah. For adults who can count. (laughs) We'll see.

Question: Well, you talked about your work with Leo McCarey. What kind—how much of an influence do you think he was in your craft?

BE: I think Leo probably was a big influence in comedy for me because when I met Leo and went to work for him, Leo was sadly kind of on the downhill side of his career. He was—I realize now—really afraid to make another movie. He went about all of the moves, hired a writer, me, and—but he really didn't want to. I guess I realized then too that he was more willing to talk than work, and so I was in great shape. I was getting a nice weekly salary and living in a terrific apartment in New York. Every day I'd get Leo talking about the old days of the business, particularly comedy and his view of what we were talking about, that kind of humor. And I remember Leo saying, "They've forgotten how to really do jokes." Of course, any old-time director is going to say of a particular era, "They've forgotten how to do this. They've forgotten how to do that." But I believe he was right in that, particularly at that time—this was a lot of years ago. What they were doing was—they were telling the joke, the punchline, and that would be the end of it. Whereas in silents, or semi-silents, with Leo—and he used this as an example—he said he shot a film in downtown Los Angeles with the old streetcars that had the fixed steps on them. And the scene was a young man putting his girl in the streetcar and saying goodbye to her and not wanting to leave her. As the streetcar picked up speed, he began to walk, to jog, and to eventually run along with the streetcar until he got going too fast for him, and the steps clipped him. He did a hundred-and-eighty-degree flip on his back. And Leo said, "Now normally that would be a dissolve to another scene or cut to another scene." He said, "But what we did was we—what I did was the young man picked himself up. He'd hurt his leg, and he was limping. He was in the middle of the street, and there was traffic that he had to avoid. At the same time when he got up, he realized that his hat had fallen off, his glasses had fallen off, and several pencils out of his pocket had spilled into the street. So while he's dodging cars and everything, he tries to pick up the pencils and put them back in the pocket. It doesn't work. And he goes through a whole routine trying to get the glasses, doing all of that. Eventually what he does is he takes—he gets, I guess, he gets the glasses in his pocket, puts the pencils in the hat, and limps his way to the curb and sits down. And normally that would be the end of it. But an old lady comes by, takes his pencils, drops a quarter in the hat, and walks off. (laughs) So it's not just topping the topper, it's topping the topper and then topping the topper." He could carry on like that. And it's a good thing to remember too, that it doesn't always apply, but if you're doing a joke, look to see if there's something beyond it, if there's a natural extension of the joke. Once you've done that, see if there's a natural extension of *that* because that's the way to get your audience rolling. That's why Clouseau has worked so well in many cases because once you start the ball rolling, you try to top it each time. You lay yourself wide open if you don't make it because you're trying to tell a joke three times, really, in a way, and each time topping it. So you better top it. And he [Mc-Carey] described what he called breaking the pain barrier. He was on the board of a hospital in New York, and once a month or once every three months or something like that, they'd all get together—I mean, the board would get together and charity cases would come in and talk about their terrible problems. Leo sat there, and he listened to one person after another come in with these terribly sad cases, each one worse than the one before. And he was really in pain after a couple of hours of this, and finally an old woman came in. She was stooped and could hardly walk, and she started to tell the story about how her husband had been taken ill and had to be put into the hospital. And how, that once he had been put in the hospital, there was no way to pay the bills, so she had to start taking in laundry. She, in doing all of the washing by hand because they couldn't afford machines or anything in those days, she developed terrible arthritis in her hands, and this began to compound itself. One thing led to another, and she got sicker and sicker. And she finally couldn't do it anymore, and about that time the husband had—or during this time—had developed pneumonia evidently, double pneumonia or something, and they had to put him in an oxygen tent. She had to do more work, and she couldn't take laundry. She couldn't do that; I forgot what she did. She was washing floors, and it got worse and worse and worse. Until finally, it looked like a ray of hope when the husband seemed to have recovered. He wasn't going to die, and he was allowed to stay out of the oxygen tent maybe for an hour each day. And she went up to see him, and he felt so good that he wanted a cigarette. He had a cigarette, took out a cigarette. She lit a match for him, and it blew him right into the next ward; there was so much oxygen. And at this point, Leo collapsed with laughter. (laughs) I mean, he began to scream and fell right under the table at the vision of this man being blown into the maternity ward. It's what he called breaking the pain barrier. There's so much you can take, and then you gotta laugh at it. Either that or go crazy, you know. And he used to talk about—he relived all of the wonderful, earlier days with Laurel and Hardy and the first great pie fight he did, all the way up to his other wonderful modern comedies. He was a wonderful character, great guy.

Question: Interesting too that he was a frustrated songwriter.
BE: Yes. Right. That's right.

Question: He always talked about the Princeton University chaplain who wrote the Princeton Triangle show and wrote a couple of songs that became standards, and his constant desire was to give up directing and become a songwriter. He never quite made it.
BE: They were a fascinating breed, those guys that grew up at [Hal] Roach in their tower out there. They won't come this way again, I'll tell you.

JP: What are the problems inherent, if any, in directing somebody you're very close to?
BE: Like Julie, you mean?

Question: Yes.

BE: Well, there's no problem. But the first time I worked with her was a problem. It's always a little difficult when the leading man is making mad love to your wife, and you're saying, "No, would you do it a little more seriously or get a little more passionate?" (laughs) Be a little objective about that. But it's nothing now. In fact, it's wonderful. We have a good time. She's a damn good actress and easy to work with and terribly professional and knows her lines and makes everybody shape up. And she's got a great sense of humor. So I can't ask for any—and I go to bed with her. What the hell's better than that? (laughs)

Question: I know you've had some problems with films being recut by studio heads like *The Carey Treatment* and *Wild Rovers*.
BE: Yes.

Question: How are you assured as a director that what we just saw here will be what—
BE: Because I have the final cut. With Orion and from now on, I made up my mind after my big problems with MGM that I would never direct again unless I could get the final cut. I was just very lucky because I left Hollywood, really never to come back and direct, to write and to lick my wounds a little bit and feel sorry for myself, while my wife raised hell because she wasn't going to allow it. I did the *Pink Panther* for Lew Grade, and Lew didn't want anything to do with the film business at that time. He was a television man, and he just thought he was getting a film for television. And so I had everything I wanted. From then on, I got everything I wanted, and I just wouldn't do it again. I worked for people—I've done many films for UA—well, it was UA, but now Orion. And I enjoy it because they don't involve themselves. They'll tell me what they think, and it's up to me whether I want to take it or not. I'm allowed to do it as I see fit, which is terrific. And it makes you a very responsible director. You work twice as hard for people like that.

Question: Well, *Wild Rovers*, I remember seeing in a theater without knowing what had happened to it. But somehow Karl Malden was listed as one of the stars, yet he was in it for like two minutes in a montage sequence. That must have been—
BE: Yes. Sad what happened to that film because I ran that film—the only other time that I've run a film in the state that you saw this one, and I knew that it was going to be cut because already the evidence was in. I ran it for Arthur Knight and his class at USC, and I told him, "This is the last time you'll see the film like this." So at least a certain number of people saw my cut, and, yes, I consider it really one of the best films I've ever made. I'm still trying to resurrect it. I discovered that all of the negative, all of the outtakes, everything, exist at MGM, and I begged them at

my own expense to let me put it back together so at least I would have the original version. No success. But there was a very important story between Malden and the sons, very important. And that led to an ending that was never there. But that's water under the bridge. (pause) Anything else?

Question: Besides McCarey, who were the other great comic directors that you admire or feel that they have influenced your work?
BE: That have influenced my work?

Question: Yes.
BE: (sighs) God, there are so many of them really. Capra. Sturges.

Question: Can you follow up on that? What particular about Capra? I don't see a relationship there.
BE: Well, I think Capra and his ability to be terribly funny, at times when things were very serious, to take a very serious—I don't mean that when you say "influenced," I don't mean that I consider that I'm Capra-like or that I'm Leo-like, McCarey-like. I mean, these are just people who I admired, I guess, and whatever I took in was not consciously. There are a lot of terrific—I mean, I love Woody [Allen] at certain times, but I wouldn't say that I'm anything like Woody. And yet I'm sure a lot of things that I see from directors then and directors now do influence me, and I'm not consciously aware of what they are.

Question: Do you think the fact that you grew up in the business because your father was in films—
BE: Well, I guess it was either do what I'm doing or be a thief and spend less time in jail—not much, but less, being a director or being a writer because that's essentially how I began, as a writer. I still feel that I am that.

Question: Well, I think one of the big influences, like with the style in comedies—
BE: Oh, yeah.

Question: There's just no way you could possibly have done the physical comedy as artfully as you do without knowing the Keystone Kops and Keaton and Chaplin and Lloyd and Laurel and Hardy.
BE: I guess I've got—

Question: All of them.
BE: Every film that Laurel and Hardy ever made. A lot of Keaton. A lot of Sennett. And I just, I don't do it much anymore. I don't have that much time, and I hope

that they eventually get on cassettes because it's a lot easier. But I love them. I just—and certainly that had to influence me, you know, by osmosis, just sitting and looking at those things because there's nothing that I have done that they haven't done. It's all paraphrasing Stan and Ollie or Keaton. Okay? Thank you.

(Applause)

BE: Thank you. Hopefully, maybe the next one, do the same thing.

S.O.B.: Do They Mean the Movie or Blake Edwards?

Myron Meisel / 1981

From *Rolling Stone* magazine, August 6, 1981. Reprinted by permission of Myron Meisel.

S.O.B.—Standard Operating Bullshit—was known for years as the film no one dared to make. Movies about Hollywood never make money, the alibis went. Besides, who wants to see a comedy based on treachery and venality? But the real question, the one nobody risked answering, was whether Hollywood would be willing to bankroll an indictment of itself.

To Blake Edwards, whose four decades of filmmaking have produced such pictures as *10*, *The Days of Wine and Roses*, and the *Pink Panther* series, writing and directing *S.O.B.* was an obsession of the most fervent sort. His assault on the motion-picture industry is the product of endless disputes with studio executives, harsh cynicism, and his ability to survive Hollywood justice by twisting its unwritten rules in his favor. There have been films about Hollywood before, but Edwards's foray is unique. The plot deals with a producer's first multimillion-dollar flop, which he tries to salvage by reshooting it as soft-core porn. *S.O.B.*'s characters are consummate stereotypes: image-conscious stars, treacherous executives, know-nothing financiers, suicidal producers, obsequious agents, deceitful lawyers, sleazy gossip columnists, feel-good doctors, and even ambitious homeboys. Edwards has made an outrageous farce, but, unlike his whimsical gags in the *Pink Panther* movies, *S.O.B.* intentionally scores laughs that hurt.

In fact, one of the delights of *S.O.B.* is imagining the consternation of movie people who will see themselves in the film. "Of course, no one can sue us," says the film's coproducer, Tony Adams. "If they did, they'd be admitting that the portrayals recognizably depicted them, and no one's pride could risk that."

With *S.O.B.*, Edwards intentionally set out to make his most personal work, to express his bright, cruel philosophy best summed up by a character in his film, *The Tamarind Seed*: "No one is to be trusted, nothing is to be believed, and anyone is capable of doing anything." This is not, of course, an attitude destined to ingratiate. Edwards is a sensitive, volatile, mercurial man, easily wounded and quick to anger. He has been known to refuse to show scripts to companies backing his production. He can often be impatient; one friend notes that "Blake will excuse himself from a meeting to go to the bathroom, and the next thing you hear is his car starting." In short, Edwards is known as a tenacious infighter and temperamental creator whose lack of love for Hollywood is normal. Nevertheless, he has been very successful in the film business, and he's aware of the irony in his comic dissection of it.

"You try, but ultimately you can't make sense out of nonsense," he says. "That's why the only way for me to approach dramatizing the insanity of Hollywood was to make a satire. I wanted to communicate not only a sense of the industry's craziness, but also some of my own since I'm a part of it."

There's hardly an aspect of Hollywood Babylon left unscathed by *S.O.B.* Even before the recent publicity about cocaine use in the industry, Edwards had barbequed it with a scene—since deleted from the final version—set in a Hollywood A party. A bald midget in livery walks about the room with lines of coke on his pate, so people snort from his head with no more excitement than they would show taking canapes from a tray.

The satire even extends to Edwards's personal life. His own doctor plays a heart-attack victim in the opening reel, and his daughter appears as a spaced-out teenage waif. Edwards even strikes against the treacly image of his wife, Julie Andrews. She was one of the biggest box-office stars in the world after *Mary Poppins* and *The Sound of Music*, but she was trapped in saccharine roles. When she tried to extend her range in 1968, playing Gertrude Lawrence in *Star!* the movie failed. Edwards suggested a vehicle that would extend and enhance the screen personality by building on her familiar persona and taking it into the realm of sophisticated romantic farce. The film, *Darling Lili*, became a legendary bomb, and Andrews didn't make another film for four years.

In *S.O.B.*, Andrews plays an actress whose career tracks her own. Known for playing nuns and governesses, Sally Miles is seen in the credit sequence in a banal musical number involving giant toys. Offscreen, Sally uses vile language, leaves her producer-husband when his picture fails and tries to guard her assets ruthlessly. Then, in the ultimate reversal of every cliché ever attached to Julie Andrews, the character agrees, for commercial reasons, to scrap her public image and bare her breasts in a hot fantasy number reshot with the same toys.

"It certainly was a meaty role," Andrews quips. "All the time Blake was working on the screenplay, he would read me the pages as they were finished. We would laugh—he always laughs at his own work—and I would assume that he'd never actually dare to make a film like that. When I first realized he would, I was terrified."

But I welcomed the opportunity to take off and let fly a bit." Which, in a nutshell, is the story of her husband's career.

Blake Edwards's family had been involved in movies for two generations by the time he was born in 1922. His grandfather, J. Gordon Edwards, directed silent features; his father, Jack McEdward, was a successful assistant director and production manager. Young Blake worked as a child actor. "It put dollars in my pocket, and I didn't think much more about it. I enjoyed the money and the certain glamour about the business, but I had no great desire to be a good actor. You could say I started out being the way Culley [the director in *S.O.B.*, played by William Holden] ended up.

"After you live in Hollywood for a while, you develop a sort of Alice in Wonderland image of the place. It's very disconcerting in the beginning—you don't want to accept how mad it all is because that becomes very threatening to your own sense of sanity. All my life I've had to cling tenaciously to my own sanity. Whenever you encounter the egos, greed and idiocy, it's always a shock, no matter how often you've gone through it. Hard as it is to accept, the business really is crazy. You want to impute rational impulses to others, but that's not realistic.

"One effective approach to coping is the path chosen by Culley. He internalizes all the conflict. Early on in his career, he decided to settle for doing considerably less than his best possible work and to seek what personal fulfillment he needed outside his work. He determines to do whatever is necessary to do his job professionally, and no more. He's a hedonist, always has a pretty young girl on his arm, and he's happy with his lot even if he tells the producer that he's out to kill himself with pleasure. I don't think he's a bad director, but he also doesn't invest his soul in his films. [The character is in large measure modeled on director George Marshall.] Sometimes I think I might have been happier if I had gone that route, but apparently it just wasn't possible for me to do so."

Edwards went into the Coast Guard during World War II and severely injured his back. Extreme pain dogged him for years afterward and may well have contributed to his tendency to inflict uncommon pain in his slapstick. As Andrew Sarris wrote of Herbert Lom's stabbing himself in the stomach with a letter opener in *A Shot in the Dark*, "There is no grizzlier gag in screen farce."

When Edwards was ready to return to work, he happened to see Cecil B. DeMille's *The Plainsman* (1937) and was moved to take some old screenplays out of his father's closet to serve as models. Following their format, Edwards wrote a low-budget western script with his friend John Champion. With Edwards acting as the hustler of the pair, they pitched the story to Monogram Pictures, then the lowest rung on Hollywood's Poverty Row. Monogram told them that if they wanted to produce it, they had better find the money themselves. Champion put up the assets in his trust fund, and he and Edwards co-wrote and produced *Panhandle* in 1947.

Edwards kept sidling into success. After hearing that Dick Powell was looking for a radio series, Edwards produced—overnight—a concept that became *Richard Diamond, Private Detective*. He went on to create both *Yours Truly, Johnny Dollar*, and *The Line-Up* for radio. By 1952, when his friend Richard Quine was given charge of a B-picture unit at Columbia, Edwards signed on and wrote five pictures, several for Mickey Rooney.

"It was the best education for me, and I also began to see the real internal workings of the studio system," he remembers. After a while, he began to direct under Quine's tutelage, starting with two Frankie Laine vehicles. On one, he remembers, he was running behind—four days over on a twelve-day schedule. Harry Cohn, the vulgar, dictatorial head of the studio, came over to Edwards in the commissary to ask why he was late. "I'm slow," Edwards sheepishly owned up. "Well," Abe Schneider, Cohn's lieutenant, noted, "at least he's honest." "Yeah," Cohn replied. "He's honest. *And* slow."

In many ways, Cohn typified the old-line studio boss: instinctive, authoritarian, poorly educated but with a gut feeling for the jugular. "Cohn operated on the principle that if he gave you your way, he'd either have the benefit of your being right or have a scapegoat if you were wrong. So if you fought hard enough for something, you could get his authorization, if not his approval," Edwards says. "To this day, for all that the style of the studio executive has changed, the need for a scapegoat in reserve is more important to them than either the commercial or artistic wisdom of a particular course." In *S.O.B.* Richard Mulligan, who plays the producer of the huge flop, confronts production chief Robert Vaughn about overbudget expenditures. "Did I hold a gun to your head to make you spend that money?" Mulligan asks. "If you didn't like what I was doing, then why didn't you fire me? . . . Fire me, and you've got no fall guy." Edwards claims this confrontation occurred substantially as written between himself and an executive during the shooting of *Darling Lili*.

After leaving Columbia, Edwards went to Universal, where he made three successful films. By 1959, he was signed to direct *Operation Petticoat*, a Navy comedy. This was the big time, and he prepared to tackle Cary Grant, whose production company was making the film.

Edwards encountered "artistic" squabbles of the sort he'd never before experienced. According to Edwards, Grant had it in mind that the submarine in the film should only be shot moving from left to right in the wide-screen frame, never the opposite; he felt audiences might become confused. "Why, do you think they'll mistake it for a Chinese or Israeli sub?" Edwards cracked. Grant was not amused. Edwards had to go to expensive lengths to redesign the shots.

On another occasion, Edwards ordered six cameras to film a scene that had to be done in a single take. The shot—a massive attack involving several aircraft and numerous extras—had been planned for days, and as everything was in motion and Edwards was about to signal the cameras to roll, he felt a tug at his trousers. "Cary doesn't like the shot," his representative advised. Mentally noting that his directing career might be over, Edwards simply ordered the cameras to start. By the editing stage, Grant had forgotten about his objections, and Edwards was not fired. The picture was Universal's biggest success up to that date, and afterward Edwards's career soared, with *Breakfast at Tiffany's*, *Experiment in Terror*, *Days of Wine and Roses*, *The Pink Panther*, *A Shot in the Dark*, and, for TV, *Peter Gunn* and *Mr. Lucky*.

Then he stumbled. *The Great Race*, made in 1965, cost an enormous amount and was disappointing at the box office. Three successive films, *What Did You Do in the War, Daddy?*, *Gunn*, and *The Party*, failed, too. During this period, he and Julie Andrews fell in love, and they embarked on a watershed project for both of them, and for Hollywood, *Darling Lili*.

The archetypal flop among big budget Hollywood productions, *Darling Lili* was released in 1970, a time of panicked financial retrenchment in Hollywood. With it, Edwards and Andrews became the touchstone for criticism of the industry's wastrel ways. The movie's failure tainted Edwards for years as an extravagant director, even though all his subsequent films—until *S.O.B.*—have met or been below budget.

The actual budget and final cost of *Darling Lili* were subjects of intense gossip at the time. Rumors pegged the final cost as high as $25 million, which at today's inflated production costs would be more than twice that amount. Edwards contends that the seven-month production was budgeted at $11 million and came in at $16.7 million; former Paramount production chief Robert Evans asserts that the original budget was $6 million, but the film finally cost $18 million.

"Paramount insisted on several factors that greatly increased the budget. To begin with, the picture was never intended to be a musical, but Paramount demanded that extraneous musical numbers be added. More important, I had priced the cost of the second-unit work [the film is a World War I flying story, with extensive aerial sequences] at $300,000 if done in the Carolinas. There were some antique planes sitting in Ireland from *The Blue Max* and Paramount insisted that we shoot there, although it meant increasing the second-unit budget to $2 million.

"That was the least of it, though. The weather in Ireland was abysmal. We finally decided to shoot whenever possible, but then we had to wait for the weather to be consistent. The sun came out, and those poor Irish faces were boiling and burning." When Charles Bluhdorn, chairman of Gulf & Western (Paramount's parent company) arrived on location, it was a beautiful day, yet the company was necessarily idle. Bluhdorn was outraged, accusing Edwards of delay.

The last straw apparently came when Bluhdorn set out on a tour of the local countryside. Looking out his car window, he asked the driver about an impressive ancient castle and who lived there. "That's the home of Julie Andrews and Blake Edwards," the driver responded. Evans remembers that Bluhdorn was furious when Edwards failed to invite him over to the castle—for which Paramount was paying—for a drink. Edwards and Evans both agree that Bluhdorn felt personally snubbed by Edwards. According to Evans, "Bluhdorn wanted to pull the plug on the production and take the loss because of the deleterious atmosphere surrounding the picture. It smelled of disaster, but I stood by the film. I think it's a damn good film, but it would have been right to have abandoned it."

Edwards, for his part, ascribes most of his problems to Evans and makes no secret that some of the material in *S.O.B.* is based on his experience with Evans and Bluhdorn. "Evans was lying consistently to Bluhdorn about the production situation, but in this business, executives often prefer to be lied to. I pleaded with the home office to get the picture back onto a soundstage—that it was getting out of control. But the executives were more concerned about having a fall guy to blame when the problems arose." Edwards feels that he and Andrews were made the scapegoats for corporate failures.

Evans denies that anyone other than Edwards was responsible for *Darling Lili*'s runaway costs. "It was the most flagrant misappropriation and waste of funds I've seen in my career," he asserted. "The primary reason the film went overbudget was his drive to protect 'his lady'—Queen Elizabeth was never treated half as well. The extravagance was unbelievable. He was writing a love letter to his lady and Paramount paid for it. He's a very good director, but terribly subjective. If he had half as much talent as he has paranoia, he'd be one of the greatest directors of all times. He had no conscience at all."

Edwards on Evans: "He had no conscience at all."

Though *Darling Lili* opened strongly in New York at Radio City Music Hall and garnered some good notices from Roger Greenspun and Vincent Canby, the film posted virtually no business after its initial run and ended up a nearly total loss.

Edwards busied himself with a new deal at MGM, which was then under the administration of James Aubrey, whose tenure at CBS had earned him the nickname "The Smiling Cobra." Edwards's first picture there was a large-scale elegiac western, *Wild Rovers*, which was intended to be a two-and-a-half-hour roadshow presentation. In that form, he believed it to be his finest work, but the studio proceeded to gut the picture, removing nearly forty minutes from Edwards's final cut. The result was an artistic abortion and a commercial fiasco.

Stung, Edwards was nevertheless enticed by Aubrey to direct another MGM project on a commission basis. After realizing halfway through production that *The Carey Treatment* would face the same fate as *Wild Rovers*, Edwards wrapped the picture as quickly as possible and fled Hollywood, he believed, forever. "I determined in my own mind that I would never direct another film," he recalls. "I intended to keep on writing, and I knew I could make a good living from that alone. I didn't see where it was worth it to fight so much viciousness and irrationality to make pictures I believed in. I was escaping, and it was necessary that I do so." During his self-imposed exile, Edwards wrote two cherished projects that he knew he had to make: *10* and *S.O.B.*

But after a hiatus of several years, Edwards returned to directing with *The Tamarind Seed*, which was backed by Julie Andrews's own production company. The movie was only modestly profitable, but its financier, Lew Grade, approached Edwards about making *The Return of the Pink Panther*. Down on their luck, Edwards and Peter Sellers agreed to reunite, each foregoing any salary up front to return for a sizable piece of the gross revenues. Made for a staggeringly low $2.5 million in 1975, the film earned nearly $100 million worldwide. Although neither Edwards nor Sellers cared to continue the series, they were prevailed upon to do a sequel, which did even better.

Sellers had grown impossible to work with, and Edwards refused to do yet another. "Peter was a great talent and a very insecure individual who could behave irrationally and arrogantly. He was inevitably a joy to work with whenever his fortunes were at low ebb, but when he was riding high with popular success, it was sheer hell to deal with him on a set. He made everyone, down to the crew, miserable. But the deal offered for the last Panther picture finally grew so alluring that I girded myself for what I expected would be the worst working experience of my life. It was, but I imagine it may well have been the best deal ever struck by a director." Then United Artists chief Eric Pleskow says, "We had to beg him to become a rich man."

Though it seemed that neither Edwards nor Sellers was capable of breakaway commercial success without the other, after their final split on the last Panther film, each went on to prove otherwise: Sellers with *Being There*, Edwards with *10* (made for Orion, the company formed by his ex-comrade from United Artists). And with *10*, the man who virtually had been banished from Hollywood as a spendthrift had made four pictures that cost a total of less than $30 million and grossed over $300 million.

Despite his success, Edwards was soon again at war with studio executives. Orion would only permit Edwards to make *S.O.B.* if he first made the frankly commercial *The Ferret*, starring Dudley Moore. After *10* was completed—but before it had opened to spectacular success—Orion abandoned *The Ferret*, even though set construction had commenced and about $1 million in commitments had been incurred.

Edwards contended angrily in interviews that he had never been advised of any reasons for Orion abandoning the project, and he speculated that Orion had done so because it lacked faith in the box-office potential of *10*. He also criticized the ad campaign as sexist and the marketing strategy as maladroit. He intimated that the company's financial circumstances may also have had something to do with its decision. Eric Pleskow, now president of Orion, and Gabe Sumner, its marketing chief, deny these charges.

"The final material submitted [by Edwards] did not meet with our approval because, in our opinion, the premise was not fulfilled," says Pleskow. "Our abandonment of the property had nothing to do with *10*. Originally, *The Ferret* excited us very much when described in broad conceptual strokes, and Blake started writing on that basis. There was no budget yet because there was no final script, and we could not definitely commit to a project until there was a final budget. As the months went by and the writing progressed, the estimated budget went up and up, but we weren't allowed by Blake to see anything he had written. We had agreed with Blake that if the film were done for a particular cost, he could do whatever he wanted. We were quite prepared to back him as a writer-director at a given figure. We liked the casting ideas and the story line, and we felt that permitting him full artistic control was a reasonable risk based on our past experience and the belief in the man as a thorough professional."

The cancellation of *The Ferret* ruptured a relationship between Edwards and the Orion executives that reached back fifteen years and eight features. "I was willing to do *The Ferret* in order to get my chance, finally, to make *S.O.B.* When that opportunity evaporated, I wondered if I'd ever make it."

But freed from his Orion commitment just as *10* established that he could still score a comedic success without Peter Sellers, Edwards was again "hot." He held his ground and insisted that his next film had to be *S.O.B.* Lorimar, an independent television production company (*The Waltons*, *Dallas*) just making a splash in feature films, decided to finance Edwards's dream.

"My comedy is sadistic," Edwards admits, "but in *S.O.B.*, it was not my goal to punish the characters. I realized that at one point, in my anger, I was even beginning to attack people who were my heroes. Of course, writing out my wildest fantasies and giving my life to my deepest fears was part of getting out the demons after all the pain I had experienced. Trying to get the picture made only brought them all out again. But I'm not sure it does much good simply to flaunt them; that's why during the course of making the film, the characters grew rounded." As savage as the final version is, it is notably less vicious than the original draft, which shocked even Edwards's old friends. "Letting the movie stew as long as it did helped the richness of the final picture."

For all his venom directed at the film industry, Edwards doesn't believe that his observations apply to that business alone. "Greed is an attribute of human nature. People are selfish. The movie business in particular attracts the sort of people who seek glamor and easy money, even when they have no apparent ability. In film, these traits are exaggerated beyond the norm, and that makes it ripe for satire. Human nature is the toughest thing in the world to change. For someone who wants to practice his art in this business, all you can hope to do, as *S.O.B.* says, is stick to our guns, make the compromises you must, and hope that somewhere along the way you acquire a few good friends who understand. And keep half a conscience."

Portrait: Blake Edwards

Jed Horne / 1983

From *Life* magazine, August 1983. Reprinted by permission of Jed Horne.

Blake Edwards swore in 1978 he'd never make another *Pink Panther* movie. He had already directed five of them. He was at work on *10*, about to make Bo Derek an American myth, make himself a mint of an $80 million box-office gross. No more *Pink Panthers*.

"CUT!"

It is a rainy spring night in 1982. Moratorium be damned. In a cobbled square in downtown Valencia, Spain, Blake Edwards is directing not one but two *Pink Panther* movies—at the same time. The first, *The Trail of the Pink Panther*, is aimed at the 1982 Christmas audience; the second, *The Curse of the Pink Panther*, at the '83 summer trade.

Edwards takes a hit of tea from a thermal Budweiser mug and waits. A snake dance of a thousand carnival extras is not quickly wrestled to a standstill. And short of human sacrifice, it's downright impossible to snuff a ninety-second barrage of Roman candles ten seconds into their run. Black gloves, stacked boots, black nylon racing jacket (Porsche)—surrounded by carnival devils and mermaids and toreadors, Edwards looks as if he took a wrong turn off Rodeo Drive and crashed *The Last Judgment* by Hieronymus Bosch.

He wants to reshoot the scene: two Mafia hoods chasing one secret agent chasing one cop chasing the dishy blond into the bedlam of a nighttime fiesta. But the skies have let loose again. Extras stampeded toward plastic canopies.

His producer and a couple of other aides hustle Edwards across the cobblestones toward shelter. Just shy of the revolving glass doors of the Hotel Astoria Palace, he shakes a fist at the sky. "Peter," Edwards whines—Job confronting his tormentor—"Peter, stop doing this to me," and he ducks into the lobby.

Boots up on the hotel bedspread, Edwards, sixty-one, reminisces about Peter Sellers. They worked together on six films before Sellers's heart gave out in 1980. He was fifty-four. "It's hard to describe the degree of the man's mental instability—given to great moods and paranoia, enormously superstitious. If anyone showed up wearing purple, Peter would walk off the set. He'd hold conversations with his dead mother at an altar he carried around with him."

Toward the end, to hear Edwards tell it, Sellers was pitching his appeals well above his dead mother in the hierarchies of the hereafter. Late one night the phone rang. Edwards had just managed to fall asleep at the end of an all-day attempt to get Sellers through a single comic bit. Exciting news: "I just talked to God, and He told me how to do it."

"Terrific, Peter." Edwards only wanted to get back to sleep.

On the set the next morning, Divine inspiration was given free rein, cameras rolling, but the results were—Edwards pauses half a beat—"really atrocious." Telling that to Sellers risked plunging him into a catatonic pout. But as the actor clambered across the set for a pat on the head, Edwards couldn't resist: "I said, 'Peter, next time you talk to God, tell Him to stay out of show business.'"

But wait. He catches himself. "I'm not one to defame the dead. I have no anger for Peter Sellers at this point."

Visitors have begun trickling into the director's combination bedroom-hospitality suite. Here's Patti Davis, President Reagan's daughter. She finished a bit part (TV newscaster) in the studio yesterday.

Edwards's daughter, Jennifer, twenty-six, had come up with the Patti idea. They were friends in a Bel Air high school. So what if Davis had no film experience. *Panther* movies are human cartoons with characterizations so broad Edwards could wring an inspired performance from his family physician—and has: five *Panthers* all told. The doctor plays the secret agent in this evening's chase and has come up to wait out the rain.

So has Geoff Edwards, twenty-three, the other child of Edwards's marriage to actress Patricia Walker. He is coauthor with his father of both scripts in production.

Only the most famous partner in the family business is missing. Julie Andrews is en route to the family digs in Gstaad, Switzerland, with Joanna, eight, and Amy, nine, Vietnamese orphans she and Blake adopted.

He has starred his wife, forty-seven, in five pictures—though never in a *Panther*. For *Victor/Victoria* she got a best-actress nomination. The director didn't get a nomination for *V/V*, but he came in for kudos of another sort. "*Vogue*, I think it was. They called me a national treasure. I've been driving Julie crazy with it: You don't mess with a national treasure."

Which only begs the question why, at a time when his options seem limitless, the national treasure is cranking out more *Panthers*. "There was a challenge," says Edwards. No doubt. Sellers alive was a director's nightmare. But making a movie that stars a dead actor . . .

Sellers was very much the star of *The Trail of the Pink Panther*, a compilation of classic scenes from earlier films, outtakes, and new sequences carefully woven around them. (Maybe Edwards's challenge told on him. *Trail* was the first *Panther* that ever came close to being a box-office disaster when released late last year.) It is a scene from the second of the two films, the just released *The Curse of the Pink Panther*, that will unfold down in the square below—if it ever stops raining. Sellers stars in this movie, too, but in a suspenseful way about which no more had better be said here.

So maybe the director is making more *Panthers* because he is in financial trouble? "Let's put it this way," says Edwards, who does not live in Switzerland solely because of the pretty scenery. "Unless the world comes to an end or banks fall, I don't ever have to work again as long as I live."

So it seems. *Pink Panther* paraphernalia, ranging from breakfast cereal to bubble bath, grossed about $110 million last year alone, and Edwards collects a licensing royalty on every last bubble and kernel of it. He also gets at least a million to make a film. Then there was the time he got $3 million *not* to make one.

United Artists in 1980 was begging for yet another Edwards-Sellers *Panther*. Still true to his '78 moratorium, the director refused. Well, then, could UA borrow the *Panther* logo for a one-shot deal? Edwards said sure—for $3 million. But Sellers died before the movie could go into production. "And I got to keep all that money." Edwards snickers the snicker of a vaudeville meanie.

In Edwards's defense, if he seems rather cold-blooded on the subject of poor old Peter Sellers, he is just as hard on himself. He makes no secret of his own peccadilloes and of the years he spent rattling on about them with a series of psychoanalysts. Now and then, his conversation shades over into the kind of free association encouraged on the couch.

"I built this model airplane. . . ." Edwards drifts back in time, trying to get at the root of an anxiety that has dogged his whole career. "I was in grammar school." That would be the early 1930s, Beverly Hills. Edwards's father, Jack, was in "the industry," as they say in Hollywood, a studio production manager, son of film pioneer J. Gordon Edwards, who directed Theda Bara in her heyday. "I took the airplane to school and one of the kids laughed at it. 'Look at the wheels,' he said. 'They're too big for the body.'"

His shortcomings as an airplane designer weren't what bothered young Blake. "I could see immediately that what he said was correct—the wheels were too damn big." But not to have spotted it first, and then to be teased by a peer. "It just validated a sneaking suspicion that I saw *everything* in a crazy way—a 'surreal' way, though I guess I wouldn't have used that word. It scared the hell out of me."

Edwards was right about one thing. The enemy was within. Dead drunk on leave from the Coast Guard—or Shallow Water Navy, as it was then known—early in World War II, Edwards took a running dive into a Beverly Hills swimming pool. Shallow water indeed. Edwards cleared the pool altogether and crashed into the far wall head first. Long Beach Naval Hospital admitted him with a broken back— and German measles. (German measles in a full body cast . . .) By the time he was discharged, Edwards had developed an enthusiasm for morphine. He was in his forties before he kicked it altogether.

With a diploma from Beverly Hills High and a handful of bit parts, Edwards figured his movie prospects were just about bright enough to warrant trying a postwar career as a body-builder. He set himself up as proprietor of a members-only gym. His partner absconded with the first year's dues.

With a trustier friend, Edwards went to see a Gary Cooper rerun called *The Plainsman*. Afterward, over a game of miniature golf, they picked apart the plot and convinced themselves they could do better—or just as well. Edwards pulled an old script out of his father's files to use as a skeleton and, over the course of the evening, fleshed out something they called *Panhandle*. Monogram Pictures was impressed enough to buy. Edwards doubled as coproducer and played the bad guy. The film made money.

By the late '50s, what with regular work writing and directing B-movies and scripting radio and TV detective shows (including *Richard Diamond* and the *Peter Gunn* series), Edwards was pulling down $100,000 a year—"which was damn flush for those days." He preferred to save not a dime. Click clothes, wild parties, and room in the garage for any sports car that caught his fancy.

With *Breakfast at Tiffany's* (1961), *Experiment in Terror* (1963), and *Days of Wine and Roses* (1963), the Edwards balloon began to rise and with it his stature in the industry as something of a favorite son (third-generation Hollywood) and a moviemaker with a patent on sixties-style cool. *The Pink Panther* (1964) and the follow-up *A Shot in the Dark* (1964) showed that he could also make money. Edwards's reputation was as glossy as any director's of his generation.

Just what happened next is open to debate—between Edwards's psychiatrist, perhaps, and a market analyst specializing in entertainment stocks. Within an unlucky seven years of the release of that first *Panther*, Edwards had watched his marriage go down in flames, lost his professional aura, and—to hear him tell it—nearly lost his mind.

The professional nadir took the form of wild and woolly fights over financing and, then, over creative control of three films beginning with the WWI musical extravaganza *Darling Lili* (1970), Edwards's first collaboration with his new bride, Julie Andrews.

Mary Poppins's career had taken a nose dive of its own as Andrews—in *Torn Curtain*, in *Hawaii*, and disastrously, in *Star!*—tried for a more sophisticated image. She had met Edwards socially years earlier—"two ships passing in the night," as she puts it. Then casting calls for *Darling Lili* rang through Hollywood. They shared career problems, an interest in psychoanalysis and now a movie set. Romance blossomed, and Blake Edwards became Mr. Julie Andrews.

He was not the only man on the outs in Hollywood. The industry was in a period of historic transformation. The old studios were being gobbled up by corporate conglomerates, and quick-footed greenhorns from the "creative" side found they could accrue the kind of power once reserved to studio tycoons by cozying up to the CPAs from New York. Overnight, men like Robert Evans at Paramount and MGM's James Aubrey rocketed from obscurity to the catbird seat.

"To give Evans his due," remarks Edwards, who says he went so far as to challenge Paramount's chief of production to a duel during the hassles over *Darling Lili*, "he later developed a kind of instinct for the industry, but at the time he was nothing but an unsuccessful actor who had a certain social association with film and absolutely no experience running a studio. He didn't know the first thing about making movies," which is a slander the rapier-tongued Evans does not suffer in silence. "He says I didn't know anything about making movies?" Evans snaps. "He's absolutely right. If I had known a damn thing about making movies, I never would have let him make *Darling Lili*—a $20 million wedding gift to his wife, and he charged it to Paramount."

Astute readers will have guessed that *Darling Lili* did not recoup its costs, though Edwards is convinced Paramount deliberately torpedoed the film to take a tax write-off.

Over at MGM, Evans's counterpart, James Aubrey, infuriated Edwards by restructuring the end of *Wild Rovers* (1971) and had begun cutting scenes from *The Carey Treatment* (1972) before filming was even completed.

"I became obsessed with killing Aubrey," Edwards now says matter-of-factly. To that end, he found himself spending a good deal of time contemplating a .38-caliber pistol he kept around the house. Then one evening as he turned off Sunset Boulevard, Edwards came a fishtail shy of running down a jogger. Regaining control of the car, he glanced in the rearview mirror, and who should have so narrowly escaped roadside retribution but his nemesis, James Aubrey. "I went into a full panic," Edwards recalls. "It was too perfect a film moment. Nobody would have believed it was an accident." Edwards finally took his revenge on the industry in his savage 1981 send-up of Hollywood, *S.O.B.*

"Five minutes, Blake." A page pokes his head in the doorway. The rain has let up.

Chase the blond: two takes. Hoods mug the secret agent: five takes, and Edwards finally gets the performance he wants from his doctor friend, who received blows to the skull and slowly sunk to the pavement in perfect syncopation with the throb of the snake dancers in the foreground.

The news spreads that Edwards has gotten enough, and, without so much as a break for beer, workmen set to dismantling lights and sound gear. It is nearly dawn, and the hour invites philosophical reflection.

Blake Edwards may have spent a good part of the last twenty years proving that he's more than Mr. *Pink Panther*. On the other hand, it does not sit at all well with him to hear the *Panthers* dismissed as a series of crude vehicles in which Peter Sellers was able to demonstrate his genius for comedy. "I know exactly what my contributions are," Edwards says a trifle testily. "And I think when *Curse* [the film with the least Sellers material] is seen, then my hand will be quite evident. Of course, it's not a matter of him or me," Edwards backpedals with characteristic vigor. "It's a question of us."

The square is now inches deep in confetti slush as Edwards heads over to where his driver has parked a rented white Mercedes. "Sometimes I think I'm just beginning to learn who I am in terms of my films," he interjects after a moment. "A little late in the day, I guess you'd have to say."

He pauses, a grin spread over his face. "Maybe I'm just the kid with the big wheels." He takes a last swig of tea and hasn't quite swallowed it when he thinks to add: "You know that kid, the one who criticized my model plane? Would you believe he became an airline pilot?"

Home Movie: Blake Edwards's *Life* Is Autobiographical

Julia Cameron / 1986

From *Chicago Tribune*, September 21, 1986. Reprinted by permission of Julia Cameron.

Movie wags are already referring to it as "Blake Edwards's home movie," and Blake Edwards isn't helping matters any. Onstage at the Toronto Film Festival's gala opening of his new film, *That's Life*, Edwards gaily announced, "I'd like to introduce my producer and my wife and kids, the stars."

That's Life is a Blake Edwards home movie. He would be the last to deny it. (It was, quite literally, shot in his own home, with his own money—$1.6 million of it—and despite its glossy production values, there is a docu-drama quality to the work. The script, all thirteen pages of it, was devised by Edwards and his psychiatrist, Milton Wexler, who is credited as co-writer.)

Jack Lemmon plays Edwards's alter-ego, architect Harvey Fairchild, a man traumatized by myriad aches and pains and, not coincidentally, his "milestone"—read "millstone"—sixtieth birthday. Edwards's wife, Julie Andrews, plays Lemmon's wife. Their kids are played by their own children, Jennifer Edwards, Emma Walton (Andrews's daughter), and Chris Lemmon.

Like *Twice in a Lifetime* and *Down and Out in Beverly Hills*, *That's Life* is a family movie. True, the family is rich and famous—"We worried about whether people would care about a family like that," says Andrews—but its concerns are those of any other American family: Are the kids OK? Will there be any grandchildren? What about everybody's health?

"Of course it's autobiographical!" Edwards says with a snort, in an interview in a Toronto hotel. "Which doesn't mean it's literal. *10* was autobiographical. *S.O.B.* was autobiographical. This one is autobiographical, so . . . ?"

"So . . . what?" Edwards is really saying, leading with his chiseled chin. A lean, hawk-faced man, sporting a black leather jacket, wash shirt, sweater, and jeans, Edwards displays a puckish sense of self-presentation that Sean Penn might envy.

At sixty-four, Edwards enjoys a well-earned and well-defended title as Hollywood's oldest Bad Boy. Even Penn will have a long way to go before topping him.

"He enjoys tilting at authority," says Andrews in a separate interview in the same Toronto hotel. Calm, direct, quietly amused, she has large, delphinium-blue eyes framed by a fine webbing of laugh lines.

Once upon a time Mary Poppins—and ever after blessed and cursed by a squeaky clean image—Andrews clearly takes a vicarious glee in her husband's shenanigans. Together, they have spoofed her own goody two shoes image. Yes, Julie Andrews does flash her own breasts in *S.O.B.*

"Blake is the stimulant I need to come out and be brave," Andrews says. "He provokes me."

Edwards provokes a lot of people. "Arrogant," "difficult," and "S.O.B." are among the nicer sobriquets tossed his way.

"Blake is so special, so gifted, so charismatic, that one forgives a lot," Andrews concedes when questioned about whether her husband's narcissism rivals that of his characters.

Not everyone forgives him.

Ever since he used his successful *Pink Panther* series to leverage creative control from the studios, Blake Edwards has been considered a troublemaker, an ingrate. Blake Edwards's rumors are to Hollywood what the smell of hops is to a beer town. There is always something sour in the air about Edwards, his newest "stunt," his latest escapade.

Just two years ago, Edwards enjoyed the dubious distinction of being the only heterosexual filmmaker in Hollywood persistently rumored to have AIDS. As it happened, he did not have AIDS—but his health was endangered. Not everyone was displeased by this turn of events. Edwards had satirized the film community too closely. There was a certain amount of glee in some circles that Edwards, that S.O.B., was finally getting his.

Why such animosity? Put simply, Edwards bugs people who play the game by studio rules. "What is wrong with him?" they wonder. "Has he no gratitude? After all the studio system has done for him?"

"To him," Edwards corrects, admitting freely that he cordially hates the studio system and what it does to artists like himself.

And what does it do?

"Controls them. Cripples them. Maims them." Edwards's voice becomes a hiss. It's clear whom he thinks the villain is.

"The *Panthers* bought me my freedom," Edwards explains. "I was desperate. I knew I couldn't go on as I had been, enduring the kind of thing that happened to me on *Wild Rovers* (a film wrested from Edwards's hands and reshaped by the studio). I needed some way to gain creative autonomy in order to keep working, and then, out of the blue, I got the idea for *Panther*. . . . Suddenly, I had bargaining power."

For many years, Edwards retained his power and used it to barter with the system: "You let me make this film, and I'll give you another *Panther*." The ploy worked very well until Edwards was lulled into forgetting what he was up against.

"I wrote a script. The best script of my life. I wrote it just for myself and put it on a shelf and it was perfect. Nobody knew about it but me and Julie and a few friends. I had convinced myself that I didn't need to direct it—that just writing it would be enough. I was trying to believe that it would be enough for me to sit in Switzerland and write. But that script kept whispering to me. That's how I found out I was a director who writes instead of a writer. The act of writing was incomplete for me."

Mellowed by his extended European vacation, Edwards forgot his need for wariness. He let a studio talk him out of the script—not that it was presented to him in those terms. Far from it. A deal was struck.

Edwards had written the movie. He would direct the movie. The studio would simply finance the movie. His deal was pay or play. In order to get him off the picture, the studio would have to pay his full directorial fee. Two huge stars became involved. They brought with them two huge egos.

Suddenly, the perfect script was no longer so perfect. Both of the stars wanted changes. The studio wanted both of the stars. Edwards's script was his no longer. The film he had planned to make himself, independently, was suddenly juggernauting through the studio mill. Still, he had a false sense of security. Studios never paid on pay or play.

But they did.

"They gave me a lot of money and told me I was off my own picture, and then I watched them chop off its hands and its feet and make it into this monster. And it was my brainchild they were mutilating."

The movie was *City Heat*, starring Burt Reynolds and Clint Eastwood.

"Take the money and run," many people advised Edwards. For a time, he would have told you that he had.

"I started another film immediately, but I had not, as I thought, transcended my loss. I had just buried it—and myself—in work. Shortly afterward, I became mysteriously ill."

The symptoms of Edwards's mysterious, much-rumored illness, he says, were "lethargy, depression, memory loss, extreme emotional and physical fatigue, hair-trigger mood swings, and exhaustion."

Like his beleaguered hero in *That's Life*, Edwards ached all over and for no apparent reason. He began to fear he was losing his sanity. For the first time in a career that has been prodigiously productive—forty-five films, thirty-six as writer, thirty-three as director, twenty as producer, many as all three—Edwards lost his appetite and, indeed, his capacity for work. His family became very frightened.

"It took us quite a while to get a firm diagnosis," Julie Andrews explains. "I was quite worried about him."

When the diagnosis finally came in, Edwards was told he had a rare, seldom publicized virus.

"CMV virus. Epstein-Barr. It's characterized by a see-saw depression. It's sort of a malarial type thing," Andrews explains.

"They don't have a cure for it. It has to just go away. You are supposed to rest, but the brain is just teeming. It makes you question everything. Blake's lasted about eighteen months."

"It ended up, finally, going into mono," Edwards says. "The idea for this film was really one of my first symptoms of recovery. I had doubted I would ever be able to work again. I was very sick when I tried to make *A Fine Mess* (his last film, done earlier this year, before *That's Life*). I don't really remember making it. I got the idea for this film—a little, personal film—and I thought, 'Maybe I could manage that.' No studios. No big deals. Just a little family film. I haven't said this before, but I don't think I could have made this film without the family around me."

Viewed that way, *That's Life* becomes a family film in a special sense. Although the film stands on its own as a movie, the sub-plot of helping "the old man" regain his confidence lends a special poignancy to the proceedings.

"If Blake couldn't work, it would kill him," Andrews says. She considered his desire to make *That's Life* a life saver at any cost.

Edwards recalls, wincing slightly at the memory, "I said to Julie, 'I have this idea for a film, and I would like us to spend our own money to make it.' To her eternal credit, she didn't bat an eyelash."

"It's a matter of priorities," says Andrews. "There are times when your family absolutely must come first."

Not everyone sees things as she does. Andrews has been closely questioned on her long-suffering-wife role both on film and in life.

"I had a reporter say to me that she thought my character was too noble and never put her own needs first. I can't agree with that. I have been lucky to be a fairly liberated lady and to do a great many things that I wanted to do."

Now that life with father is on the mend, Andrews has moved her own career back into the foreground. She will star in *Duet for One*, a movie about a world-class cellist who is stricken by multiple sclerosis.

Additionally, she will participate in a network tribute to Henry Mancini scheduled to air in October.

Asked how he felt about his recovery, Edwards cites his upcoming film *Blind Date*, starring Bruce Willis and Kim Basinger. "Three movies in one year," he says. "I would say that is a recovery."

Director—Writer—Producer—Husband—Father and Former Actor: Blake Edwards

Darrah Meeley / 1987

From *Screen Actor,* Spring 1987, p. 17. Reprinted by permission of Darrah Meeley.

Darrah Meeley: What makes a good actor?

Blake Edwards: It's the old joke: How do you get to Carnegie Hall? Practice, practice, practice. Work at your craft. Have passion about what you do, and just keep working at it. I can't think of any substitute for that. And some actors will be lucky and some won't.

DM: Do you have a technique for bringing out performances from your actors?

BE: Well, most of the time, I get good actors—that's for starters. I try to give them a sense of freedom, a feeling of responsibility, a feeling that I'm not as much a director as I am an editor about what they do. "Let's see what you bring to me. You've read the script; you know what the character is. Show me!" They'll show me, and then we start working together. I think they feel like, "Hey, what about this . . . ," and we get to be good friends. It seems to work that way.

If they're not good actors, then there's nothing you can do about it. But if they've got some talent and not a lot of experience, then you search for a way to bring out something that will be effective.

DM: You once said that you don't want what an actor has already prepared, but something that the two of you can bring out . . .

BE: I like to see what they've prepared because most of the time it's not that difficult to find good actors—there are an awful lot of them out there. If Olivier comes in prepared, I'm sure gonna listen to him!

DM: You let your actors relax so they can find some sort of creative freedom . . .

BE: I think that has a lot to do with it—getting people relaxed, so that they're not so much aware of the mechanics of what they're doing. But rather they *are* what they're doing more. Then it becomes a more real situation.

You know, they're good people. It's great to take credit for it, but listen, it's more interesting to cast Brian Dennehy as a bartender in *10* than the usual stereotype.

DM: In the sixties, you did two black-and-white films together, *Experiment in Terror* and *Days of Wine and Roses*, when color was certainly available. How would you feel if someone colorized *Days of Wine and Roses* in nice burgundy shade?
BE: Were I to do them again, I might very well choose to do it in color. I don't recall that I intentionally chose black and white because of some creative need.

But I think once the filmmaker decides to paint in black and white—how can you fuss around with that? I can comprehend what they consider to be the practical and financial aspects of it; at least, they've convinced *themselves* that it makes sense. But I think it's sacrilegious; I think it's terrible.

They were talking about it on television yesterday and showing clips from various black-and-white films, like *Treasure of the Sierra Madre*. Migod! And those cameramen! And what it took to do black and white in those days! You can't do black and white like that anymore because the labs aren't equipped to handle it, for one thing. You don't have cameramen that think in those terms—except some of the really old ones that did it.

It's just terrible to do something like that. It's like inviting everybody over to take a black-and-white line drawing of Picasso's and saying, "Let's color it in!"

DM: You made one of the first serious films to deal with alcoholism, *Days of Wine and Roses*, and now you've come out with a comedy about the subject, *Blind Date*. Do you feel that Hollywood has a responsibility to send a message about alcohol and drugs?
BE: I can talk about alcoholism because I got very much involved when I made *Days of Wine and Roses*—and I did my homework. We were in a lot of tanks and detox wards, so I know quite a bit about it. I worried a little bit about *Blind Date* glamorizing alcoholism. I think that I've been able to avoid that. It's a really tough subject, and I think we should all be committed to helping a lot.

Reconcilable Differences

Paul Rosenfield / 1987

From *Los Angeles Times/Calendar Section*, July 12, 1987. Reprinted by permission of *Los Angeles Times*.

"Us? Complicated?" Julie Andrews laughed out loud for what seemed like minutes. Blake Edwards, her writer-director husband, was down the hall in his office. When the laughter stopped, a pinch of a smile came over Andrews's face. "Frankly, I'm surprised Blackie and I have stayed together this long." Married in 1969, at the end of a decade in which both scaled Hollywood peaks, they survived *Darling Lili*, the 1970 Edsel that almost bankrupted Paramount, and resurfaced only in the '80s (with *10* and *Victor/Victoria*, among others). Even their detractors are awed by the team's survival.

"Therapy," replied Edwards, sticking his head in his wife's office. "It's our one-word answer for everything." For one five-year period Julie Andrews was in psychoanalysis five times a week; her husband has been going on and off most of his adult life, lately to Dr. Milton Wexler—who was Edwards's writing partner on *The Man Who Loved Women* and *That's Life*.

(Wexler—a former student of the fabled Theodor Reik—presides over group therapy in Santa Monica, which Edwards attends, but Andrews doesn't. At Wexler's office on a recent afternoon, the soft-spoken doctor discussed not the Edwardses but the problem with modern therapy: "For the last ten years of his life Freud spent an hour a day analyzing himself. The point was to know himself better. Now, though, there are too many therapies, too much narcissism, too much social chat about it. The question becomes: Who is stable enough to be analyzed?")

Obviously, Andrews and Edwards fit the bill. Without poking fun at therapists (as Paul Mazursky and Woody Allen have done) the Edwards-Andrews output (especially *Victor/Victoria* and *10*) reflect psychiatry in subtle ways. On consecutive afternoons of interviewing at their Century City offices, the couple was surprised to be told that Edwards had brought out Andrews's male side on screen—and not only in *Victor/Victoria*. They admitted that Edwards renovated Andrews's image. Their effect on each other is both clear and complicated.

Said Andrews, "Last year, filming *That's Life*, Blake said, 'Just be yourself.' And I was aghast. When actors say, 'Who am I?' they usually mean it. I'm not an exception. Blake makes you dig because he digs. What's happened to us as a couple borders on old-fashioned. You should see us at Gstaad." (The couple has a house at the Swiss ski village, the only place Andrews says she has ever felt completely secure.)

"I've changed, darling, from knowing you. Because I had to change. And both of us getting help is why we've changed as a couple. Look—" Andrews said sharply, her long arms outstretched, as if to punctuate her thought. "There are such discrepancies in our personalities—we are such opposites—that we had to agree on an investigation of ourselves. Blake was known as complicated and talented. I was known as sweet, in some circles, and talented. Labels are much too easy."

Is this Julie Andrews talking?

"I'm ambitious," she said strongly, "and I've worked most of my life. But I'll tell you one thing I know for sure. Marriage is the hardest work ever."

In terms of defending one's turf? Certainly this couple has different skills, not to mention different approaches. Even professionally speaking. *Playboy* once described them as Mary Poppins meets Godzilla. Whereas Andrews is primarily a *pleaser*, Edwards can be the opposite of gentle in business situations.

"It's not about defending your turf," answered Andrews. "It's about coming to terms with who you basically are. You put aside ideas of good and bad. You grow up with a certain mind set, but you change it. In my youth I longed for family life." Andrews means she went from being England's favorite four-octave teenage touring soprano to a mother with a daughter now in her twenties, and two adopted daughters in elementary school. The image of her driving in the Malibu car pool is accurate, but somehow the notion of handling Blake Edwards sounds more difficult. Andrews doesn't disagree.

"Blake has softened up," she said carefully, looking at her husband from the corner of her eye.

"OK, darling," said Edwards, verbally shadowboxing. "Let's say I'm less cynical."

"More tolerant of me, too. Last year I went off to England to make *Duet for One*, leaving Blake, who was in the middle of three projects. . . ."

Here a dilemma emerged. The one about separation anxiety. In the last decade—and even in the late sixties—Andrews had worked primarily for Edwards. As a tactic for marital survival? A way to be together? Or were those just the jobs being offered? No performer is going to say, "Those were the only offers," and nobody questions some of the Edwards-Andrews output. (In fact, his more recent films without her—apart from the *Pink Panthers*—are the most lambasted: *Blind Date* and *A Fine Mess*.)

Andrews fiddled with a finger sandwich and said, "A creative mother or wife who isn't allowed to be creative isn't going to kill her kids or eat them, but she might damn well destroy herself. So last year I did two pictures back-to-back (*That's Life* and *Duet for One*) because I'm only comfortable in my skin if I can express myself. There are years when I stopped working, but I didn't feel trapped. That's where Blake and I part company."

Edwards kicked off a sneaker and made a hard admission. "I adore this lady," he said cautiously, "but if given the choice between doing what I do and staying home and being a husband—it would not take three minutes to say I need the creative outlet more. If I had to stop working, I'd shrivel and die. Period."

Because Edwards is male, must he work? And because Andrews is female, can she take time to nurture children? Both husband and wife shook their heads.

"Forget male," said Edwards. "I just need a creative outlet. For sanity. I still need to play cowboys and Indians. Take it away, and I'm no good to anybody. I would be destroyed if I had to live without this lady, but probably more destroyed if I couldn't be creative. Without success I'd have thought of myself as a zero."

"Success on Broadway is easier if you are unmarried," added Andrews. "And Broadway-star mothers are a myth." Though Andrews is mulling over a Broadway return in a revival of Moss Hart's psychiatric musical *Lady in the Dark*, her initial Broadway period ended after her marriage to scenic designer Tony Walton and before her marriage to Edwards. For a time in the seventies, she played movie-and-TV star while Edwards played househusband, working at home (mostly in Switzerland) on scripts. Probably one day that period will emerge as a movie. Fun and games it wasn't.

"I'd come back from working all day," recalled Andrews, her voice deepening. "And Blackie would say 'Guess what happened at home today?' And I wouldn't want to hear it! I must say, though, the house was never better run. . . ."

"We play various roles in life," said Blake Edwards ambiguously.

Blake Edwards Is Up to His Movie Maverick Tricks Again

Charles Champlin / 1988

From *Los Angeles Times*, July 26, 1988. Reprinted by permission of *Los Angeles Times*.

Hollywood as the capital city of film was founded by mavericks—prospectors with hand-cranked cameras instead of mules and gold pans. And although it now dresses up like an industry, with stockholders and boards of directors, Hollywood still relies on mavericks to keep things lively and to slow the hardening of its arteries.

Reversing the usual trend, Blake Edwards, who began as an actor and then revealed gifts as a writer of often outrageous comedy, has become ever more the maverick as he has matured.

His *S.O.B.* a few years ago was a farcical satire on Hollywood itself, full of characters that seemed at best thinly disguised to protect the guilty. *Victor/Victoria* joked sympathetically about the gay life.

To make *That's Life*, a sharp-edged comedy on mid-life crisis, Edwards, wife Julie Andrews, and costar Jack Lemmon deferred most of their salaries in favor of profit participation so the film (shot mainly at the Edwards-Andrews house) could be made for less than $2 million.

"That way, if it goes, everyone prospers," Edwards said, "and if it doesn't, nobody gets hurt too badly. And you don't have to play safe with the material."

Now, on a hot July day, Edwards is shooting at a home in Brentwood, doing a scene inspired by an anecdote from the life of Sir Ralph Richardson. The film is *Skin Deep*, a romantic comedy starring John Ritter. In the scene, he is attempting to discover his ex-wife's address from his supremely hostile mother-in-law, played by Nina Foch.

Alyson Reed, a young dancer who did a dream sequence in *10* that ended up on the cutting room floor and who later won a Tony nomination for the revival of *Cabaret*, plays the ex-wife.

The film, budgeted at less than $10 million, is being made independently, financed by Joe Roth's Morgan Creek Productions, which will negotiate a distribution deal with one of the studios on the basis of the early footage.

It is not quite the family project *That's Life* was, but Edwards is again deferring much of his salary to keep the initial risk relatively small ($10 million is about half the average cost of a film at a major studio these days).

"It takes the pressure off," Edwards says. "It's bad enough dealing with one studio executive, let alone a committee. This way, as long as I'm on budget nobody much cares how long I shoot."

Skin Deep is using locations almost entirely.

"Generally speaking, it's cheaper," Edwards says. "There are drawbacks. You can't always pull out a wall, and it's not always easy to light." But Edwards, who likes to improvise around the basic script he has written, finds that locations lend themselves to improvisation.

He has a hunch that actors may not like locations as well. There are fewer creature comforts, and practical sets get very hot since the air conditioning, if any, is usually too noisy to run.

But actors, although they can take suffering or leave it alone, report they like the camaraderie and the family feeling engendered on locations.

Nina Foch, who in addition to acting now teaches student directors at USC how to work with actors and who also does private coaching, says, "Blake called me up and said, 'How'd you like to save my butt?' and then his cellular phone went dead. Very exciting." Connections were re-established, and she's having a fine time giving Ritter a hard time.

Edwards says he is writing a sequel to *S.O.B.*, in which two angels visit Earth with orders from God to destroy Hollywood unless they can find two honest men and women. Meanwhile, the Devil is doing his own recruiting.

"And where better than in Hollywood?" Edwards asks, smiling innocently.

"Sometimes," he says, "it's almost as if someone else has been writing it."

Actually, Edwards sees evidence of a new generation of Hollywood executives emerging who have the same passion about the movies that the founding moguls had.

"I can't help but admire them, even when I disagree with them," Edwards says. "Jeff Katzenberg at Disney is passionate about film; that's obvious."

"I respect anyone who knows how to make movies and cares about the business aspects as well. For a while the problem was that the studio leaders didn't *love* the business. The old guys did heavy, bad things, but they *lived* for the business. They *were* the business."

In the past, Edwards says, he has tried giving the audience what someone imagines it wants, and it usually doesn't work.

"You put the ingredients together, but it's not enough. You put *Rambo III* together and suddenly the audience doesn't want Rambo anymore. That's the mistake executives always make—looking forward to the past."

Making a movie is hard enough under the best of conditions, he says.

"I can't sleep at night. I have to take a nap at lunchtime to make up the sleep. But you can have such a good time making a film, why sentence yourself to doing one you don't love?"

Director Blake Edwards Displays a Bronze Touch

Patricia Ward Biederman / 1989

From *Los Angeles Times*, August 27, 1989. Reprinted by permission of *Los Angeles Times*.

Perhaps best known as the creator of *Victor/Victoria* and the *Pink Panther* movies, filmmaker Blake Edwards is also a sculptor. Two of his larger bronzes—*Reclining Figure* and *Interlocking*—are now on display in the courtyard between the Century Plaza Towers, part of the Third Sculpture Walk produced by the Los Angeles Arts Council.

Edwards, sixty-seven, is the first to admit that his fame as a director has boosted his recent success as a sculptor. "I'm selling a lot," said Edwards, interviewed in his bungalow at Culver Studios, which, legend has it, was Vivien Leigh's dressing room during the shooting of *Gone With the Wind*.

"I'm not foolish enough to believe it's all because it's good," he said.

Edwards knows there are some people who are interested in his work only because he is Blake Edwards-the-director-turned-sculptor. But, Edwards said, he ultimately decided that that was no reason to stop sculpting or not to show his work.

Edwards is acutely aware, however, of how much easier he has it than poor, unknown artists. "I can afford to fail all over the place," he said, "and a lot of great talents can't." With its sometimes-staggering foundry costs, metal sculpture is one of the dearest arts. "I don't know how poor, talented sculptors manage if they aren't discovered rather quickly," he said.

A lifelong painter ("I'm in the midst of a frantic watercolor thing"), Edwards did his first sculpture—a small abstract form he still has—twenty years ago. His wife, Julie Andrews, was one of his first fans.

"She really thinks I'm talented. She likes what I do, and she thinks it should be shown," he said. "I have a wonderful cop-out. It's not me. It's my old lady who is doing this."

Asked if his wife paints or sculpts, Edwards said, "No. She sings."

Until now, Edwards has painted in one of the bathrooms of his Malibu home (where the floor is impervious to art) and sculpted in the tool shed. He will soon move into a full-fledged art studio on the property. The new studio, built on a bluff, "looks almost like a wing in flight," he said. "It was expensive," he acknowledged, "but not crazy rich-man's expensive."

Self-taught, Edwards said the single greatest influence on his sculpture was British artist Henry Moore. The director recalls shooting a TV special that used Moore's sculpture-strewn English estate as a backdrop and being fascinated by the scale and complexity of Moore's huge forms. "His work was three-dimensional, and film is not," Edwards said. "It excited me that it confounded me. It excited me that I couldn't get a handle on it."

Edwards speculates that "if there is any connection between directing and sculpting, it would be angles."

The filmmaker said he finds sculpting very therapeutic. If the arts were drugs, he said, sculpting would be a tranquilizer. "I can get enormous relief emotionally from working with that clay." Painting, he said, "is joyful, but I can still get a tight gut from it."

So far, Edwards's paintings and sculptures have been well received by critics. Should the critics turn, he said, his skin has been thickened by the scathing reviews some of his films have received. "I don't like it, but I can handle it."

The Century City exhibit, which continues through January, also includes sculptural works by Gilad Ben Artzi, Betty Gold, Baile Oakes, and Charna Rickey.

Edwards said he "felt very honored" to be included. "I love that my stuff is outside, and people can walk around and see it," he said. But, he added, "The doing is what gives me the greatest pleasure."

"I Write on What I Know": Interview with Blake Edwards

Peter Lehman and William Luhr / 1990

From *Positif*, January 1990, 347, pp. 26–36. Reprinted by permission of *Positif*.

The interview that follows focuses primarily on Blake Edwards's recent career. After a long illness, his mind is swarming as usual with ideas and projects, and he is also currently working on the casting for his next film, *Switch*, which he discusses later.

Peter Lehman & William Luhr: Since *Victor/Victoria*, both the public and critics perceive that your career is declining. How do you feel about this period of your work?

Blake Edwards: I don't how to answer you. I will probably disappoint you. I'm not so sure that I changed. It's difficult for me to be objective on this subject. I'm always surprised by this kind of thing because it always seems to me that I'm able to judge my work impartially and say, "Okay, it's not so bad" or "It's good" or "I don't agree with this criticism" or "I agree with that," then continue my work without being disturbed more than necessary. But the truth may also be that not only have perceptions changed, but due to my need for experience, my need to dig into certain themes that I continue to delve and penetrate—that disturbs them, and they don't like it. You know, it's hard to say what is good or bad. I can't really judge; I can only judge what I do by a kind of primitive instinct.

PL&WL: Do you think *Victor/Victoria* is one of the highlights of your career?

BE: It's certainly a critical peak because I've had a lot of good reviews, but I don't necessarily consider it a high point in my career. It is a peak because I liked to do it and because it brought me some notoriety—a good kind of notoriety. But there are few points that I can consider as highs in my career. There are so many ups and downs that it's difficult to evaluate.

PL&WL: Has your sense of the texture of your career remained constant?

BE: Well, I think probably since *Victor/Victoria* it has suffered a bit more than a snag. It's so damned difficult, when you start talking about the creative process, to give a faithful portrait of it. I always joke about it, but it's true when I say, "I do what God puts in front of me." The way my mind works is to always play with ideas. At first, I'm still a writer, things happen, and I think, "This might be interesting." Or I stop and think and things coalesce and I say to myself, "Well, I'll work around that." Finally, most of the time, I consider myself an emotional juggler. I always have five or six things that are unclear but precise enough to juggle. At some point I throw them in the air and depending on what falls first, or what I see first, I rush ahead, because I could play this game forever, of choosing what I'll use.

PL&WL: What made you decide to make *Curse of the Pink Panther* and *Trail of the Pink Panther* immediately after *Victor/Victoria*?

BE: It was a commercial decision. And probably also, to be quite frank, to prove that I could succeed with a *Panther* film despite the absence of Sellers. I saw *Curse of the Pink Panther* the other night. It turned out that I liked it. I didn't see everything, but I thought, "Lord, it's a good film!" And I thought, "The bastards!" The fact that I sued them [MGM/AU] in court and won means something because they let the film fail.

PL&WL: It's a very subtle film.

BE: Some of my best comic effects are in this movie.

PL&WL: That gag is wonderful.

BE: André Prévin says that damned umbrella is the high point of my films for him. He says he cracked up and fell into pieces when he saw it.

PL&WL: Do you have any idea of the reasons why the concept of a series, like the *Pink Panther* films, over and over again, pleases you so much?

BE: That doesn't appeal to me.

PL&WL: No?

BE: No, not at all. Well, that's too broad. Of course, it pleases me to a certain extent. I mean, if you have something that's a success, you don't think as highly of the series as you might think. It became a series mainly because it had to, because I found that the best or perhaps the only way to get the powerful to do certain things like *10* and *Victor/Victoria* was to dangle something desirable in front of them, and it was *Pink Panther*. They believed, whenever I made one, that it would make them make a big number and a fat profit. So when I said, "I want to do 10 now," they would say, "Yes, but we want another *Panther*." So I kept it as bait, and it became a series running on its own energy.

PL&WL: Did you try to change anything significantly in each of these films? Looking back, what strikes us is that it's not a traditional series. There are so many elements that change from film to film.

BE: Yes, I always say, "Lord, if I was forced to, I couldn't just copy the previous one."

PL&WL: James Bond is more like himself from film to film than Clouseau is.

BE: And Peter [Sellers], of course, because of his passion for acting, was looking for that kind of stuff. Look at the first *Panther*, and then look at *A Shot in the Dark*. All of a sudden, in *A Shot in the Dark,* he says "meuth" and "beumb," and he discovered it between the two films. Constantly, I was looking for new material that would be a bit more original or, at any rate, different from what I'd done before.

PL&WL: Is your creativity different depending on whether you are working on another *Pink Panther* film or a *Gunn* or something in the same vein as you were doing before? Do you think you make different decisions in terms of their creative structure?

BE: Of course. It would be difficult to list these creative choices, what these structures are. It's a bit like when you talk with an old friend. There are things you expect. You can come up with a lot of interesting things because you really know each other. But if it's a brand new friendship, you pry into the corners again to see what you'll find. It's more like a feeling of surprise about new things, surprise that can lead you in certain directions.

PL&WL: We think there may be certain connections between your work and your remakes. After *Curse of the Pink Panther*, you made *The Man Who Loved Women*. And of course, *Victor/Victoria* is a remake. Have you ever wondered, Why remake something you liked so much?

BE: You know, I can use psychology, but I'll give you the facts as they are and talk afterwards. *Victor/Victoria* was brought to my attention. It wasn't what I was looking for. I didn't think, "I want to do a remake." They brought it to me, I looked at it, and I left saying, "I'm interested, but how can I get a little more interested in it—enough to turn it into a project?" It was while I was of thinking of Toddy becoming gay and playing with the homosexual aspects of that world that my interest was sparked, and I completely forgot that this was a remake. Suddenly I had something very original to me. Of course, because the film worked very well, automatically you open your eyes and ears to see if similar material could be out there somewhere, particularly European. Since you succeeded once, you say to yourself, "Lord, when I think of all these wonderful films of Truffaut . . ." You know, you play the game: "I wonder what's over there? I love so many French films. I wonder if I can draw from them?" Of course, the minute you think about it, *The Man Who Loved Women* is obvious to you, and it turns out that this is a theme that you've always thought about. You know you're like that. This was my situation.

PL&WL: Truffaut is someone whose work you admire?
BE: Yes, I love it.

PL&WL: Is there something that attracts or interests you in European cinema?
BE: Not consciously.

PL&WL: Is it fundamentally different from Hollywood's approach?
BE: Oh, yes. I think that when you speak of lots of European filmmakers, there is a quality that is certainly not inherent in this city; it's inherent in Europe and in the European spirit—whatever that means. I'm not sure what it means because when people ask me why I'm more accepted in Europe, I reply, "I don't know." I don't think I'm very European, but they say, "I thought you were English," and that surprises me. And I don't think that's just because I married an Englishwoman. Maybe it's because I spent lots of time over there. I don't know what it is.

PL&WL: The expression used by some critics is "The European art of cinema," implying that filmmakers who work in this tradition have more awareness of themselves as part of this artistic tradition, as opposed to the Hollywood notion of entertainment.
BE: Yes, I never really thought about it, but I think there's a lot of that. Just when I begin to analyze things, I get frustrated and say to myself, "I'll probably build a beautiful theory only to discover ten years later that it is totally false."

PL&WL: Is Fellini a filmmaker who consciously influences you?
BE: Oh, yes, absolutely. The first time I saw a Fellini, I found that I was very angry, irritated. Luckily, since my youth, I've learned prudence. When I get angry, when I violently oppose or am critical of something, I take the time to sit myself down and look at why I have this reaction. Nine times out of ten I wind up by appreciating it, liking or being stimulated by it, especially in art.

PL&WL: We read somewhere that this was your reaction to Jackson Pollack's work the first time you saw it.

BE: Yes, I remember. The first time I saw the work of Jackson Pollack, I said, "Shit!" And now, when you watch me paint, I'm . . .

PL&WL: You let the paint drip on the floor . . .

BE: I wanted to be different, but that's the way it is.

PL&WL: In *The Man Who Loved Women*, you play directly (we think essentially for the first time in your career) with two things that seem very important: one is psychoanalysis, the other is painting and sculpture. Did you feel it was time to confront these two things?

BE: I wish I could say that I had the impression that "it was the perfect moment." That's what I was talking about a little earlier. All my life is full of what may seem coincidences and accidents, but I'm sure that's not it. I'm sure I've been pushed in one direction or another . . . I'm sure, but it's very difficult for me to see it. When I look back, I look for the key to the mystery. I say to myself, "What drove me to sculpture?" I don't know, except that if you go back, look how I was as a child, the things I did, and the kind of things that I held viscerally, all the evidence is there. There's no doubt about that.

PL&WL: As a child, did you make sculptures?

BE: I don't think so, but I drew a lot, painted a lot. And the sculpture is the result of a slow introduction to this world that culminated in my visit to Henry Moore in his home in England, with photographs of his wonderful outdoor works.

PL&WL: Which sculptors do you admire most?

BE: Moore especially. You can see his strong influence on what I do. Now I'm trying very hard to escape it, although I don't think about it at all. Moore is someone who really attracts me. But you know, I go through phases. There was a time when I really began to appreciate the works of people as well known as Rodin and Degas.

PL&WL: Did Giacometti influence your work?

BE: At first, again, it was Jackson Pollack syndrome. The first time I saw Giacometti, I thought, "My God, what's this? What are these forms?" And one day, some years later, I was walking in a small garden in the south of France, and there were six of these figures there. I had an emotional response. I'm learning all the time.

PL&WL: In fact, we found a certain Giacometti influence in your sculptures.

BE: Very possible, very possible.

PL&WL: One of the things that intrigues us is that many of your sculptures have no eyes. They have empty eye sockets, no mouth, and there is only the sketch of a nose. The effect is very interesting. Naturally, this doesn't humanize the faces as much as one expects. Did you wonder about the reason for your attraction to these forms?

BE: No. Again, these things seem to come to me, and of course I was influenced by Moore most of the time. When you look at the works of Moore, the faces are insignificant, or sometimes the characters are faceless. This depends on what period he was in. But more and more I try to move away from this. I'm investing more time in my painting, my sculpture, and I do research. It's really funny because no one funds my research—I do it!

PL&WL: What painters do you admire?

BE: I've been painting for so long that it's hard to say. There are so many that I can point to and say that I love. I think that the only one who always knew how to touch me is Gauguin because I learned very early that he was a stockbroker who had become a painter and came to the islands and turned his back on civilization. All this touches me. Moreover, in conjunction with his way of painting, it makes me cry when I see his work, especially if it happened in the South Seas. There are also many contemporary, truly modern California artists, like Ron Davis, whom I love very much. And I love the watercolors of Nolde.

PL&WL: Is your painting as important to you as your sculpture?

BE: It goes in cycles. Sculpting, physically working with my hands, is so therapeutic. I derive such a physical pleasure, such comfort, such a relaxation that I would say that if I had to choose between them, I would choose sculpture.

PL&WL: How many hours a day do you spend on your artistic work?

BE: I can spend six hours a day sitting, kneeling, or standing on the floor of the bathroom doing watercolor because it is the only place where I feel good for it. I've been working on some oils, on acrylics these past two weeks, and I've spent more time painting than writing. I shouldn't do that. I should say, however, probably six hours a day, sometimes.

PL&WL: Even when you work on a film?

BE: Yes, and sometimes at night. I go home after the shoot, I eat, and then I'm sculpting something that drives me crazy, which doesn't leave me in peace. So I go back there, and I am able to stay outside until one or two in the morning, until Julie calls me and says, "Get back in here and go to bed!"

PL&WL: You're not credited with the scripts for *Micky and Maude* and *Blind Date* or their inception. The credits of a film can be misleading because you did much of what is called "writing" on these two films. Do you feel fundamentally different when you are working on someone else's script or on your own script? And can you explain what you do (this may include rewriting or additional pages) when you are working on a script for which you don't get credit?

BE: To become the recognized screenwriter of a film, the director, according to the rules of the Writers Guild, must write at least fifty percent of the dialogue. It is almost impossible, if you start from an already written script, to change fifty percent. But you can change it substantially. Sometimes I think back to certain films that I really changed in substance, scripts which, in my opinion in any case, could not have been shot as such. But when it came to arbitration, based on whatever criteria the Guild uses, most of the time I didn't win. I don't mention these films by name because, if I do, then I'm pointing out some writers and that's wrong. And believe me, on some of these important films that I made, I rewrote a large part of them and devoted a lot of time—as much as if I had written the original script—and I was not cited in the credits.

PL&WL: On *Micky and Maude*, were any limitations in play on what you could rewrite?

BE: The big problem with *Micky and Maude* was the ending because everyone had an opinion—Dudley [Moore] had his opinion, Jonathan Reynolds his, and me mine. And rather than going with a single idea, any single idea, which would have been much better, we made an amalgam of the three.

PL&WL: That's one of the worst endings you've shot. Is that why the film ends so quickly?

BE: I think so. You know, it just did not work. It was, I think, a really good movie up to that point. I don't even think the ending is bad, it's just not satisfactory; it doesn't work.

PL&WL: If one reads your scripts and then looks at how you work, it may seem that generally you don't have a very clear idea on the ending of your film. It seems like you had to add an ending to the script so that it's wrapped up for you to sell it to the studio.

BE: I think you're absolutely right. I think we can say that in my life. I'm really curious to discover the end—but I can't plan it! Of course, on the other hand, when I wrote thrillers for radio or for television in its beginnings, inevitably we started with the ending. We had a concept, but we always knew what the ending would be because it had to be very good, to be very satisfying with thrillers. So it's not like I've never done it. But you're absolutely right. One of the things with which I have the most difficulty is to come up with something that really satisfies me. But with the last film I wrote, I finally succeeded. It's skillful, and it's sentimental, all at once.

PL&WL: Do you feel that this time you wrote an ending the way you wanted?
BE: Yes, for the first time in a long time.

PL&WL: As you know, we found your unresolved endings a very interesting part of your work. It's very refreshing compared to those banal Hollywood endings where everything is so neatly put in its place. The conclusions of your comedies are not as strong as others.
BE: I think I like to ask questions. I like to create situations, and they don't always resolve on their own. I just finished writing a film called *Switch*; there was no way of writing it until I had the end. It's one of those films where I can't sit there and say, "It's a good idea, I'll write it, and the end will come on its own."

PL&WL: Can you give us an overview of *Switch*?
BE: The hook is very simple. You'll find it familiar, but I really pushed it a bit. It is the story of a man who is killed at the beginning of the film. Three of his girlfriends get together, drug him, and kill him like Rasputin. He doesn't go to paradise but stays in limbo—or what's between Heaven, Hell, and Earth. God says to him, "On one hand, you're a great guy, and you have acquired enough credits to enter Heaven. On the other hand, you have been so rotten towards women that I'll send you back to Earth. If you find a single woman—that's all, only one—who loves you, I'll let you in Heaven." He says to himself, "Great, I have a second chance. I can go back. How hard is it to find a woman who loves me?" Then he wakes up in his bed the next morning and says, "It's a new day. I'm still alive!" He gets up to piss, and, of course, he still doesn't notice he's now a woman. Now he's got to find this woman, but no longer as the man he was before. I had a lot of fun with it, but it also had me begging, and it scared many people in the trade. Many people at the beginning told me, "I will do it, but you have to remove two sequences because the average American is not ready for that." I said, "I can't do it." I thought about it, then went back and said, "If I don't do them, then it's over for me. I would rather not make this film than take out these two things."

PL&WL: Is it the backbone of the film?
BE: Not really. The actress I wanted had the script and told us that she liked it, but for various reasons she couldn't do it. I suggested taking out those two sequences

to see her reaction, and she said, "If you take them out, I won't do it." I said, "That's a point in your favor. You realize that they might doom us." She replied, "If you don't take the risk . . . I'd like to do it because it's different. I'm dying with laughter, and then you suddenly throw me off a cliff." It's true I cause her to be raped, to get pregnant, and to give birth. He schemes to get a job in an advertising agency. He asks his boss, who doesn't realize that he's a man in a woman's body, for a job. He claims to be the sister of the guy. The boss says, "Why should I hire you?" And he replies, "I'll get you the big account." "You get me this account," says the boss, "and the job is yours." Now the guy knows that the woman responsible for the budget in question is a notorious lesbian—beautiful, intelligent, etc. Then he thinks, "I'm a woman now, I can seduce her." And because he's reacting as a man, he doesn't think there's a problem. After all, my God, it's only a matter of taking a woman to bed. Then begin some big complications because he wants to control everything, but he's a very beautiful woman. I play with that. At first, all the money men said, "The average American! Lesbianism!" and so on. I said to them, "If I can't play with that, then I'm out."

PL&WL: Homosexuality and lesbianism usually appear in your films with secondary or minor characters. You usually introduce these gay characters not without unpleasantness at first glance. For example, Toddy's situation at the beginning of *Victor/Victoria*, where he is exploited by the guy he lives with. And in *Skin Deep*, where the manager is bitter and acerbic, and later on at the reception one discovers that he was preparing to die. In *10* also, you have the relationship between Robert Webber and the young man, and in *Sunset* there's a lesbian relationship. In most of these films, there's an element involving this kind of unpleasant exploitation and at the same time you are compassionate. You make sure the public identifies with some of these gay characters. Is there ambivalence in your mind about homosexuals? Is there an element in the narrator that partly wants to punish them and make them unsavory and an element that wants an audience to really identify and sympathize with them?
BE: In the first place, it's part of sexuality. Whether they're gay or not, it's sexuality that interests me.

PL&WL: This is essentially the real question of your films.
BE: Yes, that's the real question. And I've known so many homosexuals, so many people in this world, and my perception of this world, probably very narrow, is that—for some reason, I will not try to justify or explain it—many gays that I knew in Hollywood or in the entertainment world were very intelligent, terribly creative, and very crafty. I saw this especially in New York. They call it the gay mafia, where the gay world actually controls the theater, and uses its sexuality as

a cruel weapon sometimes. For me, they are very interesting to portray because of certain excessive elements in their personalities. One of my close friends, who was my dialogue assistant, was a dear, adorable fellow who had that sort of spirit and language that constantly tore down the whole community. This made sense because they were so critical of him and because God knows what he endured in his gay life. I think one has to defend the rights of everyone to choose their lifestyle, but I also think I have the right to say what I think, to say things that I constantly see. I can't be clearer.

PL&WL: Instead of showing homosexuals as weird, as they are in some movies, you show them as people who have relationship problems like heterosexuals do.
BE: Of course, because they have them!

PL&WL: But your films polarize them: there are homosexuals and heterosexuals. With the strange exception of transvestites in *Gunn*—and this seems the exception that confirms the rule—have you stayed away from bisexual characters in your films?
BE: I think so, because I don't understand them. I have no contact with them. I don't know any bisexual. I mean, I certainly am aware of them, but I don't know them. You understand? I've never considered bisexuality in my lifestyle; I've never been sensitive to it. I've always been fascinated by the homosexual world. I find it infinitely harder for me to comment on bisexuality than on the two extremes.

PL&WL: The gangster character Fusco in *Gunn* can be seen as a bisexual because he has relations with Daisy Jane.
BE: Yes, you're right, by God. I never thought of it. Of course, you're right.

PL&WL: Only in a strange way, because we recognize that you set it up after the fact. He's really a transvestite murderer; he's not presented as bisexual, at any point as the film unfolds.
BE: But you see, I don't know how to represent him as bisexual—unless he stops to tell you that he's bisexual. With a real homosexual, I can use some clues to make it apparent, and with heterosexuals it's obvious, you know!

PL&WL: It's very interesting, with all the mythology about sexuality in Hollywood, that you don't know anyone who is bisexual.
BE: It's one thing to come out and say, "I'm gay!" I don't know anyone who comes out and says, "I'm bisexual!" I've never heard it! I think the bisexual world is easier to hide, protect, or even ignore than one extreme or another.

PL&WL: So don't you think it's more threatening in some way?

BE: I don't believe so. It's just that I don't understand it. I remember when Julie and I were interviewed by *Playboy*, and the reporter said, "I'm going to talk about a thorny issue. You know, there are rumors that imply that Julie and you are . . . ," and he meant bisexuals, that we were having sexual exploits, and things like that. I just looked and said, "I won't comment on that. If you had said, 'I heard you were homosexual,' I could have said, 'Okay, let's talk about it.'" Or if he said that Julie was a homosexual, that would have been ridiculous. But when he implied that we were bisexual, I said, "That's too complex for me." I'm not looking at that kind of sexuality.

PL&WL: Why do you think you're perceived that way?

BE: Oh, I don't know. It is so typical of this city. There has been this rumor that I have been a homosexual since I started in this business, and nothing is further from the truth. I don't say this to boast. In fact, to those that traffic in this, I say, "Listen, if you want to discuss it, I can only tell you that if I were gay, I would be the first to admit it. I'd spill the secret and say, 'I'm gay.'"

PL&WL: Before we leave the subject of directing others' screenplays, let's talk about *Blind Date*.

BE: I did a tremendous job of rewriting this film, and there was an automatic arbitration—not because I rewrote it, but because Leslie Dixon, Dale Launer, and others like them are the original authors. It's interesting that Dixon told you she made so many objections to the revised version.

PL&WL: She said that.

BE: She's not in the credits.

PL&WL: It's an ironic situation. But the script that her agent sent us says, "Written by Dale Launer, edited by Blake Edwards, Leslie Dixon, and Tom Ropelewski." In any case, Dixon and Ropelewski are not credited with the film.

BE: My feeling is that I have nothing to do with the script, but maybe I'm wrong. All I know is that there were things I found unacceptable that I didn't want to do. I don't know if that has anything to do with it, or if it's Launer, but I remember that the drunken girl's mouth slips toward the guy's fly, then she vomits on her knees. These are not things that particularly interest me. Those types of things are what I changed.

PL&WL: Is it true that you added the entire last part?

BE: When they throw him out of the house? Yes, it's true.

PL&WL: Apparently, there used to be a short scene where they get married, and that's it. Then you added this big comedic section, in Blake Edwards's style, where all these people come in and out of the room. That's an excellent example of a major change that you made and for which you weren't credited because it's a long passage without much dialogue.

BE: That's true.

PL&WL: Talk about *A Fine Mess*. In some physical comedies, particularly *A Fine Mess*, you have minimal thematic development. We don't find a theme in the film. You set a baseline as a framework, then virtually ignore it to develop a remarkable sequence of gags. Is this how you structure physical comedies?

BE: It's hard to talk about this film. I remember its genesis, but I don't recall how I arrived at this structure. It's like asking, "Can you describe for me your two years in the insanity wing of a psychiatric hospital? Give us references and hallucinations!"

[Note: Blake Edwards was sick while directing this film.]

PL&WL: Many people say that in movies like *A Fine Mess*, *Blind Date*, and *The Party*, there is no character development and little plot; the characters go in circles, they're frantic, and there are all these elaborate gags. For example, in *The Party*, Peter Sellers shows up and trashes the guy's house for an hour and a half—there's not much more than this. And in *A Fine Mess*, there's this chase for an hour and a half.

BE: That's your way of telling the story. You can lose an hour and a half or two making something interesting to bring to the screen for me. Some choose to make *Lawrence of Arabia* with character development and everything that makes up these films. But I think you have to ask yourself, "What is the purpose of what we're doing?" Do we have to stick to this serious narrative, to the development of the characters? I remember what inspired me to do *The Party*. Talk about Jackson Pollack throwing paint on a canvas, and you'll get "How can he do that, it's not art!" This happens all the time, across the ages. Not that I'm this great innovator, but what drives me to do things is that suddenly I like things. I think, "Lord, that could be fun! Wouldn't that be different?" I don't think about whether or not I develop the characters or plot. *The Party* emerged from the fact that so many things in *Panther* with Sellers came from discovery, spontaneity, going off on tangents; things that weren't written and that were done on the set. I don't know why. I said to myself over and over again, "Wouldn't it be fun to make a whole movie this way?" The *Panther* films revolved around this. This doesn't mean that you can't have serious plot, interesting characters, and development. We've only chosen not to do it this way. We're great admirers of the first films and their simple plots.

PL&WL: It was a clichéd saying of critics, after seeing *A Fine Mess*, that it was a short film stretched into a feature film.

BE: Perhaps so. Who says you can't make a short film? If it doesn't hold your interest, if you don't laugh, then you've failed. But if people laugh and like it, then you've succeeded.

PL&WL: Have you watched *A Fine Mess* since you made it?

BE: Yes.

PL&WL: Did you like it?

BE: I think that it's better than people said it was.

PL&WL: Whether it worked or not, essentially it's a movie where one enjoys the frenzied layout of all this humor. There's no reality to the characters nor thematic development. But it can be a treat if the film is otherwise structured—which seems to be the case here. You put a lot of energy into structuring those gags.

BE: Yes, and I like that. I always come back to the fact that it's not that bad! It's even pretty good.

PL&WL: What brought you to produce *That's Life!* independently? Was it because no one wanted to finance you?

BE: I don't know whether or not someone would have done it. I think I just didn't want to deal with the usual problems. I think I wanted to control everything for a change, to know what it feels like to put up one's own money, and to do all these things. I was in the Jacuzzi one day, and I started to feel better. The illness left me, and I thought, "I want to get back in there and do something that won't put me under so much pressure." The best thing was not to stay away. I'm a man attached to family. I make a family everywhere I go, and I always have the same people working with me. My family, Julie, the children, and all these things are so important to me that I thought, "Let's put my family and my professional life together and make a movie." Maybe it's not a very adult way to act but I've never been an adult person.

PL&WL: To promote the film, you said it was highly autobiographical. When you look back now, in spite of all the brutal frankness, is there any case where you think you left some things off the table? Is it both frank and deceptive?

BE: I don't think it was misleading, knowing then that we would have to be able to make a four-hour film. I think that perhaps in terms of the time I would need to develop it. If I had decided to do a miniseries, I would probably have given up a lot.

PL&WL: We don't mean "give up" in this sense. You're certainly very critical in many ways about the character that embodies you. Are there areas you repress, saying, "I'd criticize my hypochondriac side or my womanizing side, but, God, I won't do this or that?"

BE: No, I think that if I had only dealt with this character, I would have been much more tempted to study my other facets, or his. But since it was her story as much as his, I didn't have time to do more than deal with the main elements—the hypochondriac, the womanizing side, that sort of thing—and I played with it the best I could.

PL&WL: *Sunset* was a project you thought about up until you finally directed it with Bruce Willis. When you have a personality as well-known as Bruce Willis, do you need to redefine the project?

BE: Oh, yes! I think that happens quite often. It definitely happened in the case of *Sunset*. The original casting of *Sunset* had Jimmy Garner and Robert Duvall. They would have played Tom Mix and Wyatt Earp. And when you feel Duvall in the role of Tom Mix, you can see the difference between the two.

PL&WL: There's a huge difference.

BE: Duvall wore this role like an old coat and would have shown the true western side of Tom Mix because Tom Mix was actually a cowboy; he was a sheriff. When Bruce came in the film, he had to become a more artificial Tom. It was important to show this urbane side of Bruce, whatever he did. So this character had to be changed, and the relationship between Mix and Earp then became very different. Now one represented the West and the other Hollywood, so they could no longer have the same kind of close relationship as in the original concept.

PL&WL: Don't they have an age gap too? Duvall is middle-aged while Willis is a young man.

BE: That's true, absolutely. One would have had more of a feeling of contemporaries with Duvall and Garner. This had to be transformed from the young man to the older man. And all these things had to be put in place.

PL&WL: Are you satisfied with *Sunset*?
BE: No.

PL&WL: Can you explain the reasons why you're dissatisfied?

BE: I think I exhausted myself to do it. I couldn't have done otherwise, and then Bruce arrived. I really thought it would work, but I failed. It might have worked, but I couldn't get there. I might have done so with Duvall.

PL&WL: *Sunset* doesn't have the visual sophistication of most of your other movies. It's rather flat. The camera work and the editing are less interesting than usual. Apparently, when relationships between the characters started to break down, the film also lost the visual vitality you usually bring to your movies.

BE: I can give lots of reasons for that. I won't talk about the main reason because it concerns the personalities and the problems we had. Historically, these things don't necessarily bother me. But so many unpleasant things came from the production company, and that kind of thing, that I think it was inevitable that I would lose my enthusiasm or even the ability to do it properly.

PL&WL: Throughout your career, and particularly recently, you've taken people with a star image and cast them against their type. You said you did it with Craig Stevens in *Gunn*. Bruce Willis had a totally different image from the one you gave him in *Blind Date*. George Carlin's image was much more raw than his character Justin Case in the television show. And John Ritter, whom you had in *Skin Deep*, had a well-defined television image that differs from his role. It's more than just casting against type; it's reconsidering a career and launching someone in a new direction. Did you think of it this way?

BE: Yes, and I think that if it works, it's an additional quality. I was very impressed with an example of this when I was younger, and it was Dick Powell. It's like a return, a rebirth. This is about being at a low point, finished, and suddenly getting up and getting back in shape. I like to think that my career is full of that. Earlier you were talking about what the critics were saying recently. In a sense, this is one of the things that pushes me to work harder, to study and come up with something that says, "Well, now be hypocrites." Now I'm back with *The Return of the Pink Panther*. I'd like to hear you all say, "I knew you would do it!"

PL&WL: But John Ritter isn't really finished."

BE: That's true, but there are elements of this. Ritter was finished in movies. He's still a great, great television personality, and, I think, he prefers that. He didn't want to fight to make films, and I understand that. He had his chances in film with Bogdanovich and others, and it didn't take. But I don't think he's an extreme example like some of those who you named. Think of Powell singing *By a Waterfall*, and suddenly his career stops until he makes *Murder, My Sweet*. Suddenly this guy you saw on the screen with Ruby Keeler becomes a tough guy with short hair. In any case, this worked, and from that point on he's more constant, more credible. This gave him something that you wouldn't get anywhere else. Bogart is like that. Nobody thinks so, but Bogart was once "the handsome young man." He was first a young lead before playing Duke Mantee.

PL&WL: Did you see John Ritter's television work? Is that the reason you picked him?

BE: I had known John for a long time, and, yes, I saw his television work. As a physical actor I always liked him, but I knew things about him beforehand. When we started the casting and his name came up, I said, "I thought about it, but I think he's too young. He's kind of a cherub." Then Tony Adams, my producer, saw him on television and said, "He let his beard grow; look at him." And when I saw the beard, I said, "Let's go!"

PL&WL: Is a key function of this film to highlight a surprising aspect of the character for people who saw him on television in *Three's Company* and *Hooperman*?

BE: Yes, and I hope that same phenomenon works for *Justin Case*.

PL&WL: Putting George Carlin in a Disney movie and choosing Peter Strauss for *Gunn* seems to be a first. In these cases you worked over and over again with actors in roles that differ from their star image.

BE: The thing you're talking about doesn't always work because at first I didn't see Strauss as Peter Gunn.

PL&WL: You mean that the script was written before you chose him?

BE: Yes. I didn't think of him at all. He was one of the actors acceptable to the network. It was really a commercial choice. I'm glad it was Strauss because I like him, and I think he did something on par with what you were pointing out. But I didn't choose him for that reason; I didn't think that way. I can't remember what the reasons were for George Carlin.

PL&WL: Many people think of him as outspoken.

BE: I still have to say, "Pay attention to the truth." The real Justin Case was harder, more frightening, much louder, in a way, than what you can do on television. It wasn't meant to be a Disney movie, not at first. At first, there was no suggestion that he act like an old bastard towards the girl.

PL&WL: Was it a theatrical performance originally?

BE: No, it was planned for television but after 9 p.m. Suddenly, it turned into this Disney thing and was toned down and became benign.

PL&WL: That's the perfect word. This is a benign version of some of the ideas you play with in your other films. When you make a pilot for television, do you use a different outline than the one you use for movies? Do you look at seven or eight things that will be carried throughout the story as important enough to be mentioned in the first episode?

BE: Obviously, you hope to know the time slot for which you're writing because it is essential. If you write for 8 p.m. or earlier, you're limited to certain things. The Commission is going to kill you. You can only do some of the things I like to do. And if it's after 9 p.m. it depends on the channel because at NBC you can do more than ABC.

PL&WL: What about the character of the young neighbor in *Justin Case*? Is the reason why you spend so much time on her that if it becomes a series, she will be a colorful character to bring back week after week?

BE: Absolutely, that's it. You learn very early on television that you can't hope that your actor will be in the show week to week, so you start positioning the show in a different direction. You have the main characters to carry the episodes, and very often these people leave to kick off their own series. So you have to take that into account.

PL&WL: These two recent television movies are sexually conservative.

BE: Certainly, yes. Watch the TV movie *Gunn*—it's because of the network. It's that simple. You're caught up with that.

PL&WL: But is there no way to innovate without displeasing the network? For example, at the end of *Justin Case*, the woman is totally trapped by these powerful men in a way that is so atypical of your films. It's interesting to compare this film with *Victor/Victoria* because in *Victor/Victoria*, the woman is more challenging. This woman does only what George Carlin's character tells her to do, eventually moving into his home. There is no indication of her stifled feelings or that she speaks of herself as the character of Julie Andrews in *Victor/Victoria* does. It's very light, but the same situations would be much more complicated in your movies. And in the television film *Gunn*, too, this sort of material is not nearly as challenging as in your films.

BE: No, actually. Again it depends on the time of broadcast, it depends on the network, it depends on a lot of things, and you're caught up with that, most of the time.

PL&WL: We started this interview by saying that a critical perception of your work is that *Victor/Victoria* is your best work and that your films have since declined. Another critical perception that one often encounters is that your films are more and more concerned with the problems of the rich and the privileged. Have you become unbelievably interested in people whose lifestyle is extremely privileged?

BE: I don't think I'm more and more interested. I think there are several answers to that question. One is that if I worked at the speed most directors work, we wouldn't be having this conversation because I wouldn't have made as many films as I did. Then, when you have so many movies to watch, one after the other, certain directions seem to be infinitely more obvious, more glaring. Another answer is that I'm certainly not the first to write about these people. And it's also probably because I know people like this much better than I know the average family that might have the same problems. I'm not intimately concerned with the average family; otherwise, I think I could write about it. Another answer is that I write comedies. You know, I try to make hits with people. One critic said, "Who cares?" But does it matter if a film is successful? I would like to say to him: "I hope you don't get cancer or writer's block because you're very privileged, and I'm sure you have an easy life. If that happens to you, I wonder if you would think we should give more consideration to the middle class than to successful people." I think successful people who have problems are equally interesting. Maybe critics don't give them enough importance. Maybe I don't give them enough importance. I can understand how this can be a valid criticism, but I think it's just bullshit. I can quote a lot of artists who focus on a theme, sculptors and painters who go through a period when they repeat themselves, trying to do better and better. You know, you become obsessed with something, and you want to do the best you can with it. I think it was Vincent Canby who criticized me, saying that one of my films was as if I was someone who never left California. And Woody Allen, good God? What should critics say? Is it as if Woody Allen never left New York?

PL&WL: It so happens that New York is where he lives.
BE: Yes, but California is where I live! Here is where my roots are. I could make my objections, but certainly I disappointed Canby somehow. I angered him somehow; that's why he attacked me. Well, let him go fuck himself! I don't care. I get angry because I think it's not on the level.

PL&WL: The people who acquire this importance are usually white. How do you react to the subject of minorities in your films? You have a tendency to have racial minorities in minor roles. For example in *Skin Deep*, there is an oriental servant in the house. Have you thought about that?
BE: You mean: give them major roles rather than minor roles?

PL&WL: Or just drop them, rather than give them minor roles.

BE: No. I mean, I certainly do not want to drop them. I'm deeply concerned about racial problems. I've always been. I was one of the first to try to break this racial barrier on television when I asked Ricardo Montalbán to do *Mr. Lucky*, and I fought the channel. Montalbán was my first choice, and I encountered racial prejudice. "A Latino as a star? Absolutely not!" They were not going for it. My antiracist commitment is much less visible in terms of what I think and what I do. To give you an example, at one point I wanted to do something that would be a real contribution to the racial problem, but I thought, I cannot write a black movie. I'm not black. And then I have to avoid it because I'm going to wipe out if I try something like that. So the best thing to do is put someone in my movie who would be the best friend. He's not the leader; he's the second role or something like that. But then, I always write about a black person and to do so I think I should go find a black person and say to him, "Work with me on this. I want to know how you think." Anyway, if a black person doesn't do that, it will never sound right to me.

PL&WL: It is a virtue of your style, in fact, because there is a kind of simpleminded liberalism that says, "I speak for blacks," or on any subject at all.

BE: That's the most dangerous thing in the world.

PL&WL: There is no sense in speaking on behalf of other people. If it turns out that you are famous, a privileged white man with your way of life, this is the core of your experience. You can't think that you have to prove your good intentions towards blacks or any other minority. It's the same with homosexuals; they have minor roles in your films because your interests are elsewhere.

BE: If I were to write *Boys in the Band* or something like that, forget about it! If someone says, "I want you to describe a homosexual lifestyle," I would say, "I can give you a brief picture, but I can't go beyond that. I can only give you what I observed. I didn't experience it." And so, when I thought, "I'd like to make some kind of contribution," I wondered, "how can I, as a director, do it?" I had an idea, and I put it down in writing. I always wanted to do it, but I never did. I can always still do it. I timidly called it *Negative*. I thought in terms of film, positive and negative, the negative of an image. I began the narrative with a riot like Watts. But you suddenly realize that the rioters are white and that the power is black.

PL&WL: That's a reversal.

BE: I did everything in reverse because I could write from the point of view of the white people. I gave them a patois. I did everything. And I thought, "Wow, this is going to fuck up some minds." You know, some of those Southern reactionaries who identify with whites—their biggest prejudice is color—who hardly care about anything else intellectually. If you're black, tan, or yellow, it's an automatic prejudice. So consciously or unconsciously, they compare themselves to the whites. While they defend the whites, in my film the white man says, in a sense, all that the black man says. That will fuck them up.

PL&WL: Rather than speaking for other groups, you show the contradictions and problems of the privileged white male.

BE: You know, it might be braver, but I think it's more prudent. I am what I am. I write about what I know.

Jimmy Smits and Blake Edwards— *Switch*'s Real Men

Daniel Schweiger / 1991

From *Entertainment Today*, April 12, 1991. Reprinted by permission of Daniel Schweiger.

Usually it's females who have to combat macho stars for screen time, but *Switch*'s wacky twist is to have a man-turned-woman take control of her fellow actors. Ellen Barkin is Steve *and* Amanda in Blake Edwards's newest comedy, a sleazeball who's murdered and given a second chance as a shapely chauvinist pig. The straight man for this reluctant sexpot is Jimmy Smits, effectively contrasting his *LA Law* image here as an uncertain ad exec who makes a play for his best friend's "sister." By the end of *Switch*'s uneven, yet engaging bed-hopping, both men behind and in front of the camera would come to a better understanding of their masculinity.

"I admire actors who can go from comedy to drama and are equally good in both genres. Like them, I don't want to play it safe," Smits remarks in his hotel room, anxious to hear the reception to his first lead in a romantic comedy. Best known for his impassioned TV attorney Sifuentes, the adorable Smits has had an equally engaging, if far less popular, film career. Starting with a murderous drug kingpin in *Running Scared*, Smits has played a cursed cop in *The Believers* and a head doctor in *Vital Signs*. Unfortunately, nearly everyone missed his impressive portrait as a tormented revolutionary in *Old Gringo*, a slight that he's hoping *Switch* will rectify. The character of Walter might have offered less dramatic possibilities than Smits was used to, a light role that the actor thought Edwards wouldn't see him in.

"I knew the part was going to be a big hurdle when I first read *Switch*," Smits comments. "Walter's like Anybody USA, and I knew my name wasn't on the first-choice list. But it was to Blake's credit that he let me come in and read for the part. The vibes were good, and he gave me the shot. I can't say that I wasn't nervous about *Switch*, but if you're going to do a comedy that's based on physical timing, you couldn't be luckier than to have Blake Edwards behind you. I'm a big *Pink Panther* fan, and there's lots of funny stuff in his body of work. Blake knows how to make you laugh with the right camera shots, so all of that anticipation was quickly wiped out."

Working with a tough guy like Ellen Barkin also insured Smits's performance, changing conceptions about his sex and the nature of acting. "I always try to be more communicative in terms of feelings. Men are brought up to contain their emotions, and I really want to let mine out on a daily basis. Walter has the 'good guy' flag since he's the counterpoint of the other male chauvinists. The relationship between me and Ellen was also buddyish. A running joke was calling Ellen 'M'lord!' whenever she walked on the set. She was there for fourteen weeks in practically every scene. We all have bullshit meters that ring out whenever something doesn't sound true, and there was realism in everything else that she did. Ellen is totally honest and calls it like she sees it. I really admire that in people, regardless of their gender."

As Amanda challenges Walter's ideas of how a man should behave toward the "fairer" sex, Smits hopes that her lesson won't be lost on the audience. "The good thing about *Switch* is that you'll laugh a lot but at the same time question your opinions. Walter finds out a lot about women, especially because Steve treated them so badly in his past life. He finally believes Amanda's story when the coincidences pile up and understands that Steve is inside this beautiful package."

Smits's appearance as Walter and his role as a freed Cuban prisoner in the coming *Fires Within* completes his switch from television to film, a decision marked by his exit from Mackenzie-Brackman on the show. "Leaving *LA Law* is a new chapter in my life, and it's especially difficult because I love the show and its family atmosphere," Smits remarks. "People often ask how the program turned me into a role model, and while it's good to speak out on certain issues, that image can limit your choices. Because of Sifuentes, I could never appear in something like *The Silence of the Lambs*. However, *LA Law* will leave a door open for me. If they choose to have Sifuentes fall down an elevator shaft, let's just say there will be a net at the bottom!"

"I don't want to be the star in every film," Smits concludes. "I just want to do good projects and work with good people."

Blake Edwards has never had a problem with getting talent. The legendary director of such comedies as *Breakfast at Tiffany's*, *S.O.B.*, and the Inspector Clouseau series, Edwards has employed such slapstick geniuses as Peter Sellers, Jack Lemmon, and Robert Preston. The past decade has seen Edwards's wild tastes turn to such sex-role farces as *Victor/Victoria*, *10*, and *Skin Deep*, their heroes' potency thrown into disarray by demanding women. It's a feminine mystique that's been spurred by Edwards's marriage to Julie Andrews, whom he cast in drag for *Victor*. "I'd say that *Switch* continues *Victor*'s themes," he remarks. "I understand men because I'm one of them. But women have been an enormous puzzlement.

They've created a lot of ambivalence in my life, with pleasure and angst. I find it worthwhile to investigate them."

With Ellen Barkin and Jimmy Smits, Edwards found actors who could embody his gender confusion. "We all start out as something undefined with the potential for going in either direction. Chromosomes determine if we become male or female, and Ellen was in touch with that masculine side. Besides, I'd hate a movie without an attractive leading lady to get my heart started in the morning! Jimmy got across a confused, little boy quality that was needed to redeem Steve and Amanda."

Edwards used a collaborative approach for *Switch*, mixing the actors' opinions with his raucous imagination. "There's a lot that influences me on an unconscious level, and I leave my creative ear open and watch whatever floats to the surface. I don't try and figure out where they all come from. I just know there's a reason for them. That allows me a great amount of latitude when I get on the set. A scene I may be in love with is never engraved in stone, and I find that actors are very bright and tremendously instructive. If you give them an area that isn't restrictive, they'll surprise the hell out of you."

Switch might start off as a breezy satire, but it soon twists into unexpected dramatic areas once Walter drunkenly seduces Amanda and results in a bizarre lecture on date rape. Their night also brings *Switch* into the abortion debate. But where Amanda's decision for her child is explicit, Edwards shies away from the equally interesting, if far less tasteful seduction. "I didn't want to show it because the movie was already treading a very fine line," he says. "It would have offended the audiences' sensibilities, and everyone who read the original script took exception to it. The backers wouldn't make the film unless that sequence went, and I'm convinced that I made the right decision.

"I knew the abortion issue would be just as tricky," Edwards continued. "I'm totally for women's rights, particularly on that issue. But I have some kind of strange way-down-deep feeling for the other side. If the choice was mine, I'd have the baby, and that's the approach that Steve and Amanda would take. What's happened to him will never occur to another 'man,' and Steve wants to see it through. One of the things that drove me to write *Switch* was to show what it's like carrying a baby. I have two kids by one marriage, and I felt like a total outsider during the birthing process. It suddenly becomes your wife's world, and I always wondered what her experience was about."

Though he's best known for *Switch*-type slapstick, Edwards is hoping to return to drama with *Henderson the Rain King*, a Saul Bellow adaptation that will be far less humorous to get off the ground. "Although most of my films haven't lost money, they haven't been blockbusters either. Combine that with the fact that I'm a renegade, and you're going to have problems raising money from the establishment. Since I'm not a big fan of Hollywood's powers-that-be, I'm left to do projects independently, and that's the way I prefer it."

Whether *Switch* is a box office hit-or-miss, the film's rambunctious style confirms that Blake Edwards is the last practitioner of sixties-type comedy, based on an outrageous premise, strong characters, and outlandish physical comedy. "I wouldn't define myself that way," Edwards counters. "I have a lot of trouble trying to categorize my approach since my genesis goes back to the screwballs. I don't want to come up with a theory for comedy; I learned it from all those brilliant people who made me laugh as a kid. They've allowed me to manage life by seeing humor in unpleasant situations. Even Laurel and Hardy had it tough."

His Pain, His Gain

Kirk Honeycutt / 1991

From *Los Angeles Times/Calendar Section*, May 5, 1991, pp. 5, 23–27. Reprinted by permission of Kirk Honeycutt.

In Blake Edwards's comedies there is pain in every pratfall.

Dudley Moore, in *10*, hiding amid a floral display in a church during a wedding, gets stung by a bee. Herbert Lom, Inspector Clouseau's neurotic boss in *A Shot in the Dark*, stabs himself in the stomach with a letter opener. Richard Mulligan, the failed movie producer in *S.O.B.*, attempts to hang himself on the second floor of his house only to have the rope break, sending him crashing through to the first floor, severely maiming a Hollywood gossip columnist.

The pain, Edwards makes clear, is autobiographical.

"I would not be able to get through life had I not been able to view its painfulness in a comedic way," he says. "So when I put [life] up there on the screen, quite often it resembles things that happen to me or at least comic metaphors for those things.

"Leo McCarey [the late comedy writer-producer-director] used to talk about breaking the pain barrier, where you're faced with so much pain it compounds itself and you can't take it anymore. So you laugh."

In his bungalow on the Culver Studios lot, relaxing on a recent afternoon on a sofa with his feet on a coffee table, the sixty-eight-year-old director gave the appearance of a man at ease with himself and his film career, which spans six decades.

The appearance can be deceiving. It belies a life of continual physical and emotional pain. That pain inevitably turns up in his films' dark humor.

Friday, Warner Bros. will release *Switch*, Edwards's forty-eighth film as a writer, director, producer, or a combination of all three.

In *Switch*, a womanizing ad executive (Perry King) is murdered by a trio of furious ex-lovers and is reincarnated as a woman (Ellen Barkin). With his male soul—and libido—trapped inside a woman's body, he finds himself flirting with a lesbian cosmetics magnate (Lorraine Bracco) while fending off the advances of his best friend (Jimmy Smits). Familiar Blake Edwardian themes all—mortality, role playing, and sexual confusion.

The world Edwards portrays is often a heartless, chaotic place, with potential for destruction as well as creation. It falls to his characters to straighten out the chaos and make sense of the nonsense.

"What Blake does is comedy, but there's so much sadness in his characters," says John Ritter, who starred in Edwards's *Skin Deep*. "The man who gave you *The Pink Panther* is mixed with the man who gave you *Days of Wine and Roses*."

Edwards's physical pain can be traced to a dive he took into a swimming pool while serving in the Coast Guard during World War II. Too much alcohol and his unfamiliarity with the pool resulted in a fractured skull and broken neck. What happened as he lay in a traction cast for five months at Long Beach Naval Hospital perfectly illustrates his theory about the pain barrier.

"I nearly died. Lying in that hospital, I watched them bring these poor bastards out of the Pacific, shot to hell in sea battles, and I looked worse than anybody. 'Jesus,' they'd say, 'what happened to you?' I couldn't say that I dove into a Beverly Hills swimming pool. I'd groan and turn away.

"It was hell, right to the day I woke up and saw Eleanor Roosevelt, standing at the foot of my bed, where she said those terrifying words: 'What happened to you? Where were you wounded?' The whole ward erupted in laughter.

"Stories like that I've somehow been able to turn into life's funny moments."

That particular funny moment has resulted in a chronic bad back that, according to his close friend, composer Henry Mancini, who has scored twenty-six Edwards features, can act up "when things get tense."

His emotional pain, though, began much earlier. Edwards grew up with parents he terms "dysfunctional." There was not much love "because they didn't know how [to love]. I don't blame them although I did for a long time."

Edwards's natural father left his mother before he was born. After his birth, in Tulsa, Oklahoma, his mother turned him over to an aunt and uncle. When he was three, he moved to Los Angeles, where his mother had remarried. For several years, he shuttled between Tulsa and LA.

"I was raised by a flock of women—all very well intentioned—and a Pennsylvania Dutch uncle who was secretly very generous and kind but couldn't express it. My stepfather was not much different."

As an only child with parents who could communicate neither with him nor themselves, Edwards felt "the only way I could communicate was by throwing a tantrum."

He escaped his unhappiness at the Saturday movie matinees. "I naturally embraced the Laurel and Hardys, the Keatons, and the great comics. I laughed and made my hours there happy. I could take a certain residual of that home with me."

Edwards says he didn't meet his biological father until he was forty. "I thought he was dead. He'd been a phantom through my life. It was a very interesting experience—an unfortunate experience. I never should have opened that Pandora's Box.

"I couldn't feel much for him, but he suddenly wanted a relationship with me. I couldn't provide it. It became very sad. I had to face it one day. I said, 'Look, why didn't I ever hear from you?' He could never really answer—just a lot of corny speeches. I said, 'I'm not angry at you. I just don't buy it. If you buy it, you'd better resolve it yourself, or you're never going to be happy.'"

Edwards's stepfather, Jack McEdward, was a successful assistant director and production manager. Young Blake worked as a child actor but treated this first exposure to moviemaking as a lark. After the war, that attitude changed. He needed a job.

So in 1947 Edwards co-wrote and produced with a friend *Panhandle*, a low-budget Western that starred Rod Cameron and—for the only time in his career—Blake Edwards.

Thus was launched a career that has certainly been one of the most checkered in Hollywood history. His early hits in TV—*Peter Gunn* (114 episodes) and *Mr. Lucky* (34 episodes)—and in film—*Operation Petticoat, Breakfast at Tiffany's, Experiment in Terror, Days of Wine and Roses, The Pink Panther, A Shot in the Dark*—were followed by a trio of fabulous movie disasters.

Darling Lili, made for Paramount in 1969 and starring Julie Andrews, who soon became his wife, was that era's *Heaven's Gate*. Its very name became a code word for an extravagant director going wildly over budget. Edwards places the blame with the studio's insistence on adding musical numbers and shooting aerial combat sequences in Ireland where weather was terrible. His next two films at MGM, *Wild Rovers* and *The Carey Treatment*, were taken away from him and brutally cut by studio head James Aubrey.

Edwards fled to Europe. "I banished myself. I said I'm leaving, not coming back and not going to direct anymore. It hurt too much. I was too angry and depressed."

Then, quicker than you can say Pink Panther, Edwards was hot again. Edwards and actor Peter Sellers, both down on their luck, agreed to reunite to make another film about the bumbling Inspector Clouseau.

The Return of the Pink Panther was followed in quick succession by *The Pink Panther Strikes Again* and *Revenge of the Pink Panther*. All were huge hits. All caused, says Mancini, "a great deal of pain for both Peter and Blake."

The two men didn't get along. Yet, as Edwards acknowledges, "we had a common field of comedy dreams. And probably, if I had to admit it, we shared a certain child-like quality. The child in both of us was very domineering and powerful. The difference was I knew it, and he didn't."

When the two finally split, Edwards's career continued its rebound with a trio of his best comedies—*10*, *S.O.B.*, and *Victor/Victoria*.

Despite contracting a chronic-fatigue virus eight years ago, which Edwards describes as "like ongoing mononucleosis," he has continued making nearly a movie a year. Not all have been successful, however. Or don't you remember *A Fine Mess* and *Sunset*?

Along with the silent comics he enjoyed as a youngster, Edwards's cinematic and comedic forebears include Leo McCarey, Preston Sturges, Frank Tashlin, and Billy Wilder. Jack Lemmon, a close friend and star of six of his films, remarks, "I don't know a director better at visual comedy than Blake. He's the best I've ever worked with at what is *not* shown on the screen."

Lemmon points to a sequence in the *Panther* series in which Clouseau comes into his flat anticipating an ambush by his servant-cum-martial arts instructor, Cato (Burt Kwouk). When none is forthcoming, Clouseau draws a bath. Moving in and out of a stationary frame, he starts water running, removes his clothes, dons a robe, and disappears into the bathroom. A moment later, Cato runs through the frame and into the bathroom.

"You hear a horrendous splash, a scream, and see water shoot out the bathroom doorway," recalls Lemmon. "Ninety-nine percent of directors would have hired two stunt guys, and you would have seen one guy fly through the air and land on the other. It would not have been as funny."

Edwards helps actors by finding greater interest in their work than his camera angles, says Ellen Barkin. "Doing an Edwards film is much more akin to doing a play. You don't do two lines of dialogue and go to a new angle. If you watch his movies, he treats the set like a proscenium. There's not a lot of close-ups, but actors moving in and out of shots."

Sight gags and physical confrontations abound. The slapstick, critics have noted, springs from the frantic attempts by characters to find order in an absurd, anarchic world. Edwards's heroes ultimately learn that order must come from within. This is often accomplished by modifying their self-image. Thus, Edwards is frequently preoccupied with role playing, especially sexual roles and stereotypes.

In *10*, *Victor/Victoria*, *Skin Deep*, and *Switch*, Edwards seemingly equates survival with the ability to explore ambisexuality.

"I've always been totally fascinated by the opposite sex. Because I've had an interesting life with women and been very introspective about myself and how I relate to women and they to me, I've pursued this theme.

"In the beginning, I didn't think it would be as obsessive. But the more I tried to figure it out and dramatize it, the more I discovered that one two-hour film was not enough. I'm very much focused on my own feelings and confusions I have about the roles we play, both male and female, and feelings we deny."

JoBeth Williams, who costars in *Switch*, notes that Edwards "has enormous compassion for people stuck in roles they may not be comfortable playing. In his own life, he has chafed under the masculine role he had to play. You can see he feels it somehow screwed up things, and he resents that. Blake feels that if we can get in touch with the opposite sex in ourselves, we will have greater understanding and communication between the sexes."

The compassion and insight Edwards has brought to his several portraits of gay life may partially account for rumors that he himself is gay. He has continually denied this, most recently in an interview in the April 23 issue of the gay magazine the *Advocate*, saying, "If I were gay, I'd be the first person to step out and say so."

The headstrong nature of his heroes is another autobiographical element. Throughout his career, he has squabbled with studios and executives over everything from meddling in his artistic vision to marketing. (Orion's ads for *10* he called "vulgar" and "sexist.") Nor has he been shy about filing lawsuits.

"He's a loon," remarks an agent who has dealt with Edwards on occasion. "He wants things done his way and expects to be treated as somebody special. But he's in a position to expect it because he is a major creative entity."

Of his feisty personality, Edwards says, "It's my character. I'm not sorry about it, but I do regret the energy wasted."

Edwards says that he has not so much mellowed as found ways around confrontations, which didn't prevent him from filing a $25-million lawsuit in February against MGM-Pathe over the studio's refusal to finance another *Pink Panther* film with Gerard Depardieu playing Inspector Clouseau's illegitimate son.

This combativeness apparently doesn't carry over into his work with actors or crews. "I fell in love with making movies with Blake," says Richard Mulligan, who has appeared in four of his films. "It's a very relaxed, easy day. He comes fully prepared, but he embraces anything you come up with."

JoBeth Williams appreciates his behavior toward women. "I always felt he took me very seriously as a person. Some male directors look at you like a sweet little actress—do your job and shut up. Blake treats women with high regard and interest."

On an Edwards set, practical jokes abound, actors say. Lemmon reports Edwards drove studio head Jack Warner crazy while making *Days of Wine and Roses* by shooting innumerable gag scenes he had no intention of leaving in the final cut.

"Afterwards, I realized making such a heavy drama about two people who were roaring drunks would have been unbearable without his practical jokes."

Certainly, the relaxed practical joker on the set is at odds with his emotional life off the set.

Edwards has been in psychoanalysis or therapy for a good part of his adult life. He even wrote two scripts—*That's Life* and *The Man Who Loved Women*—with his analyst, Dr. Milton Wexler.

But it was at a group therapy session about a dozen years ago that he says he received the biggest shock of his life. In listening to the sad story of a highly successful woman whose life in many ways paralleled his own, he came to the realization that his own life, to that point, had not been worth the struggle.

"That was a horrendous shock to me, a moment of truth. I thought, 'All those years and it wasn't worth it?' I went home about as depressed as I'd been in a long time. I then faced the issue: OK, are you going to dwell on the fact everything up to now hasn't been worth it or get on with trying to make something of the time you have left?

"Of course, the answer was to try to make something out of life so at the last moment, if asked was it worth it, I'll say, 'Well, maybe.'"

Asked to give a progress report, Edwards says he's "getting closer to the maybe. I have more forgiveness, more humanity, maybe greater bouts of depression as a result, but I'm beginning to see just a glimmer of what I consider to be what this [life] is all about. In the final analysis, I really am the master of my own destiny."

For Edwards, true happiness may lie in burying himself in work. Presently, he is trying to launch a film based on Saul Bellow's novel *Henderson the Rain King*, for which John Briley (*Gandhi*) has written a script, while simultaneously preparing to direct the first six episodes of *Millie*, his wife's TV sitcom for Viacom and ABC.

Then there's his family life. Along with their grown children from previous marriages, he and Julie Andrews have adopted two Vietnam War orphans who are now teenagers. He and his wife are actively involved in Operation America, an international relief agency, and charities dedicated to helping children.

It's obvious in talking to Edwards and those who know him that his wife has been the stabilizing influence in his life.

"Julie doesn't stand for any b.s.," he says. "She won't let me get away with things like my hypochondria. She's a tough one to follow. But you either follow or don't. And there are too many interesting things about her that make me want to keep following. She's very steadying. She's my main sail. I've been running around with jibs and spinnakers most of my life."

Edwards stops dead, astonished at what he's said. "I've never used that analogy before! Where did that come from? I'm not a big sailing man. But she is my main sail—you run that big sheet up when you need steadying. She's my big sheet."

How will his wife react to reading his description of her as a big sheet?

Edwards smiles. "Just make sure you spell it right."

Topping the Topper: Blake Edwards

Raffaele Caputo / 1991

From *Cinema Papers*, no. 85, November 1991. Reprinted by permission of Raffaele Caputo.

Leslie Halliwell once wrote of Blake Edwards, "a man of many talents, all of them minor." This is perhaps the standard view of Edwards among many critics, particularly Anglo-Americans. He has been described as one who showed a great deal of promise early in his career, but mid-way through had somehow run out of creative energy. But considering his film career goes as far back as 1947, well within the studio era of Hollywood, and that he has dealt with an industry that at best can be described as volatile, Edwards proved to be a most durable filmmaker. This is made evermore sharper given the near-catastrophic result studio intervention on *Darling Lili* and *The Wild Rovers* had on his career in the early 1970s.

Edwards certainly represents the generation of old-school auteurists yet is still working in today's Hollywood with relative independence and integrity. His latest film, *Switch*, starring Ellen Barkin and Jimmy Smits, is the story of a man who becomes a woman but not by his own volition. However it may be received, publicly and critically, there is enough evidence to show his career is not about to end. But even if it were, as though Edwards could be analogous to a blazing comet on the verge of burning out, then it is apt to quote from *S.O.B.*, "But ah my foes, and oh my friends, it gives a lovely light."

Raffaele Caputo: Role reversals and confusion of sexual identity are not uncommon features in your films. Do you think you have exhausted the possibilities with *Switch* [1991]?

Blake Edwards: I probably have in terms of emphasis, of doing a whole film about [role reversals]. These kinds of things might crop up again, but only incidentally and not as the major portion of a film. In my early ones they turn up as well, so maybe they're evolutionary. But I am not really a student of my own films. People tell me these sorts of things are there, and I say, "Oh, that's interesting." I suppose they do crop up to some degree, if I can rely on the critics. There has been a couple of books written, but I can't remember the names of the authors off-hand.

RC: To use the title of the song from *Darling Lili* [1969]—"Whistling in the Dark"—your characters in *Switch* emerge from the darkness, literally and metaphorically, given they are "in the dark" about their sexual identities. What is Steve Brooks [Perry King] in the dark about, or, for that matter, Amanda [Ellen Barkin]?
BE: That's a very interesting question. I don't know that they are in the dark before the transition is made. He doesn't have any problems initially and knows pretty much who he is. But when he becomes her, she is certainly in the dark about a lot of feminine things. He/she has to learn. Because it is convoluted, I guess you could say that he is very much "in the dark" throughout the whole film, to one degree or another, as to what women want. It takes becoming a woman to find that out. That's the way I would describe it.

RC: One really isn't sure where to draw the line, but a key moment in *Switch* is when Amanda is about to make love to Sheila Faxton [Lorraine Bracco] but doesn't. It's pointed out that she might be homophobic, but actually it's Steve Brooks who is homophobic.
BE: Yes, I think Brooks is very much homophobic before the change happens. He is an insensitive womanizer and as unpleasant as I could make him, short of turning him into a serial killer. He is a man who suddenly becomes a woman and has to struggle with that situation. He is homophobic to the degree that, even though he is in a woman's body and is faced with the possibility of having an affair with Sheila, which at first is interesting to him because he regards it as a kind of masculine prerogative, he's saying, "What the hell, I have a woman's body [but] I'm still a man in my head, so I'll have no problem. I'll just lay her and that will be that." But when he gets right down to it, the homophobia that he suffers from is so great that he can't manage it.

RC: And the curious thing about *Switch* is the unlikely combination of a "high-energy feel" (like in *Blind Date*) and then probing a dark mood (as in *That's Life*). In your later films, dark elements creep in at unexpected moments.
BE: What you're saying is absolutely true. It has that probing element, but it's neither the high-content nor high-energy type. It's a little of both. I can't talk too much about it, but I like to feel that people think not whether they're good or bad but that they evolve. Again, whatever I do has some evolution to it, and it's moving ahead. I don't know whether "ahead" is correct, but it doesn't stay static, anyway. There is a dark side to this film, no doubt about it.

RC: Could it be related to the fact that, although your films always have a central figure, you're not so much interested with establishing the [character's] individualism as with the relationships of a group of people? The individual is important for you but not as a beacon of the group, rather as someone who sets off relations to see what is the social embroidery.

BE: As you are making these observations, I'm trying to adjust to them and ask myself, "How true is that?" I know you have a point, definitely, because there is a very strong social point of view in my films and maybe to the exclusion of the characters somewhat. I have been trying to think of other films, and something like *Victor/Victoria* [1981], which certainly talks a lot about role-playing and things to do with social-sexual roles, is a very strong character-driven piece. Since then, however, the character-driven aspect is maybe less discernible. I don't know. It's hard to respond because, while I recognize what you are saying, I don't recognize it so strongly that I can really address myself to it without a lot of thought. It's so fucking hard trying to. I mean, I enjoy an interview like this because it provokes me a little.

RC: Let's look back to some pivotal films in your career: I think *Experiment in Terror* [1962] and *Days of Wine and Roses* [1962] represent two radical departures from the types of films you were making previously.

BE: It's interesting because I always believed for quite a while that one didn't necessarily have to be typecast as a director. I probably predicated that opinion on the fact that I did get for those films you've mentioned, and certainly for *Wine and Roses*, some high degree of praise as a "serious" filmmaker. That's just to use a word. Not that I believe comedy can't be serious because it is very serious at times. Strangely enough, and I don't know whose fault it is, whether mine or the industry's, I seemed to be pushed into the mold of being a comedy director. And it's a very, very rough industry at times for a filmmaker to try something else.

I have just finished a script which is a very dark piece. I was quite excited about it, naively so. I gave it to my agent, and he didn't care for it. He sort of suggested what I should do next or can do next. In other words, if he were to go out and sell me in the marketplace, he wouldn't have a chance of selling me for one of those films. I felt myself getting really pissed off. I always believe, as Billy Wilder said, "You're as good as the best thing you've ever done." And I think some of the best things I've ever done have been, if not a whole film, then moments of very serious stuff. I hope so, anyway.

So, I resent the fact that what my agent said might be true. It makes me really irritable, if not angry, because right now in my career I'm infinitely more important in Europe than I am in the United States. I can undoubtedly go to any number of European countries and make films until I can't get out of my wheelchair.

RC: Why do you think that might be?

BE: I don't know. You naturally tend to say, "Well, it's because Europeans are less smart or more discerning than us." You find yourself playing that little game which is not good. The only thing I have been able to come up with is that it seems Europeans are more interested in filmmaking. They are more interested in the process of making a film and in the people who make them, the auteurists. When I am interviewed by the European press, as opposed to the American, or even when I talk to people in Europe who may not have anything to do with the industry, but are filmgoers, they really seem to know so much more about it. They don't just go and sit there. I'm sure some do, but there is an awful lot who seem to be interested in film and the people who make them. They can be just as discerning about something they don't like as what entertains them.

In the States, there is a kind of spoon-full-of-sugar mentality. People go to be entertained. How the film got there, and what is behind it, is really of no consequence to them. I really can't figure it out, unless somehow I've become European by osmosis. I've spent so much time living in Europe, and I'm married to an English lady [Julie Andrews]; maybe I am unconsciously more European. It's possible.

RC: *Gunn* [1967] is another pivotal film, more than anything else because of the dialogue. Take the exchanges between Peter Gunn (Craig Stevens) and Jacobi (Ed Asner), the dialogue there is sublime . . .

BE: I don't remember the sequence that well. What I can say is that I came out of radio, where all you had was dialogue. I also grew up on Sam Spade and the Dashiell Hammett genre, which I truly love. I don't know how but somehow I gleaned a little of that for myself.

Although these days we are able to tell very good stories and make some wonderful films without much dialogue, we're forgetting that there are theatrics in what we do. I enjoy the theatrics. But with such an emphasis on naturalism—and there's nothing wrong with that—somehow the theatricality is lost.

I'm delighted that you feel that way about *Gunn*. It was not a film I had intended to do. It was a kind of low-budget movie my company was supposed to do. I had written the script, but then I had to step in and replace the director. It turned out to be great fun.

RC: Of all your other films, *Darling Lili* is probably the most intricately devised in terms of the way the appearance of the characters keep switching—is this a mask or the real person?

BE: That's very interesting. *Darling Lili* is one of those films that drives me crazy because it came to represent a major turning point in my personal life and my career working for a major studio. Unfortunately, I didn't have final cut, and my prerogatives were usurped by a new regime that moved in. It's an old story by now, and people around are kind of tired of hearing it. I tried to do certain things with that film which I think would have made it a much, much better movie. So, for me anyway, there is a part of it that is a wonderfully disfigured beast. It has such interesting mood changes—the things you were talking about. But it's hard for me to even describe. If it had been done today, it would have won, or certainly been nominated for, any number of Academy Awards. Like the cinematography, look at the original print of that film and show me somebody from that year that even came close to that kind of cinematography. We worked so hard to get such wonderful things from a great cast, the sound recording, and particularly the art direction and costumes. There is no doubt in my mind that film deserved half a dozen Academy Awards, leaving me aside. If they had allowed me to do certain things that I wanted to do, I am absolutely positive it would have been a commercial success. But they just destroyed it. Yet there still seems to be enough left there to make me sad, so it seems they really didn't destroy it completely. But I wish they had gutted it totally.

RC: *S.O.B.* [1980] is a most damning and dark film. No one or nothing gets away unscathed, except the dog . . .

BE: That was a result of *Darling Lili* and another film I felt was the best I had ever done and which I had to let the studio completely destroy. It was called *Wild Rovers* [1971], a film I loved dearly. If you have to see that film, please get a hold of the long version; it's closer to the version I wanted. And if people do see it, I'd love to hear from them just to hear what they think about it. I truly mean that.

RC: The slapstick tradition is very strong in your films. Possibly because of that, a good deal of critics tend to slot you into a light-weight category. But much of your comedy is also highly sophisticated. Take for example in *Victor/Victoria* when King Marchand [James Garner] discovers that Victor [Julie Andrews] is actually a woman, and even though he seems secure in his heterosexuality, he is actually hiding inside a closet. It's a subtle kind of humor that makes us laugh at ourselves, at our fears . . .

BE: I don't think that was my intention. I don't set out to say, "Okay, I'm going to make my audience laugh at things." What I set out to do is exorcise my own demons, to make myself laugh at things which, to one degree or another, represent other people. That's the way I approach it, and sometimes it works and sometimes it doesn't.

RC: You just don't use a gag and throw it away; you really milk it. *The Party* [1968], for instance, even though it has been described as episodic, is really one continuous gag from the moment Hrundi V. Baksi [Peter Sellers] comes through the door with mud on his shoe.

BE: I'd love to talk about that. I learned that technique through a very famous director named Leo McCarey. I was a writer then, working for him, and he taught me a lot. We'd sit, and he would talk about how filmmakers had lost the art of the visual joke. One time he was describing to me a scene in one of his early two-reelers where a young man sees a girl off on a street car, and in those days in Los Angeles the street cars had fixed steps. So, anyway, she's up in the car, and he's standing in the road talking to her. The street car begins to move, and he begins to walk along with it. The street car gets faster, and he's walking faster and faster. Eventually he begins to run alongside the streetcar, and it is going so fast that the steps flip him 180 degrees and he lands on the street.

Now that would be the joke today. But not then, however, because now he has the problem of getting out of the way of traffic, and when he landed his hat flew off and all of his things fell out of his pocket. So he has to not only dodge the traffic, he also has to retrieve various things. The best way to do that, he figures, is to put everything in his hat. When he's done that, dodging traffic all of the time, he gets to the side of the road and sits down on the curb. A lady then comes by and drops a quarter in his hat. That's the end of the joke.

I've always remembered that story. Whenever I do a joke, I always investigate to see if there is a topper, and, if there is, a topper to the topper. That was what we did with *The Party*. It is a very innovative film, and I love it.

The Clouseau Gene

Jerry Roberts / 1993

From *The Hollywood Reporter*, October 22, 1993, T-14, T-16. Reprinted by permission of Jerry Roberts.

Rebelling against being pigeon-holed as a comedy director, Edwards talks seriously about drama, humor and "breaking the pain barrier." Blake Edwards was interviewed by *The Hollywood Reporter*'s Jerry Roberts by telephone at Edwards's home in Switzerland.

Jerry Roberts: As the Preston Sturges Award recipient this year, your distinguished work on both sides of the hyphen is being recognized. Can you pick one vocation over the other?

Blake Edwards: How can I? Before I became a director, when I would go to another country and go through customs, the airlines handed out little cards for you to fill out. I wrote *writer*. Now I write *writer-director*. But the great thing about being a writer is that it's not limited to a soundstage and equipment and a crew of people. I wrote *S.O.B.* in the middle of the Alps. I wrote a western—*Wild Rovers*—right here, looking out the window at these mountains [the Alps].

Roberts: Your grandfather, J. Gordon Edwards, was a well-known silent film director who directed many of Theda Bara's vehicles. Did they have any influence on your career?

Edwards: I've seen a two-reeler. That's all. Most of his films were destroyed in a Long Island fire. [So] he was not an influence. But my father certainly was. He was an assistant director and production manager—mostly for Fox. His name was John "Jack" McEdward. No *s*. The family name is McEdward. He worked for Fox from the late twenties to just after the war. Subsequently, he worked as a production manager for me on a number of my films—up until fifteen years ago. His last film was, I believe, *10*, which we made in 1978. He passed away at age ninety-four. He worked hard all his life.

Roberts: Critic Andrew Sarris once wrote that you seemed to follow in the foot-steps of Billy Wilder in the tradition of American film comedy. Can you comment on that and talk about other directors you admire?

Edwards: Before I ever decided to become a director, before I knew Billy, I considered him a mentor. He was as strong with drama as he was with comedy. *Sunset Boulevard* and *Stalag 17* are great dramas. Others who have influenced me would include Preston Sturges, Ernst Lubitsch, Willie Wyler, and Orson Welles. Peckinpah, of course. Richard Quine was one of the best directors around. I also like Stanley Kubrick very much and, lately, Robert Altman.

Roberts: Though your name is associated with comedy, your filmography includes *Days of Wine and Roses* and other films outside comedy. Does it bother you that you are identified as a comedy director?

Edwards: It sure does. You can be typecast as a director just as an actor can be. Most of this comes from the great success of the *Pink Panthers*. And I love how successful those movies have been, but this is a complicated issue with me. I've always been a loudmouthed rebel where the establishment is concerned. I say loudmouthed, but I would like to think there's intelligence backing that up. And if you are this way, you're sometimes forced to get pictures made without support. So I didn't get a lot of opportunity to direct drama. The studios didn't give me the opportunity. I couldn't stand their ethics. And even more than that, I couldn't stand their lack of creative judgment. It all just excluded me from doing drama.

Roberts: Your reputation as a maverick has been reflected in your movies about Hollywood, particularly in *The Party* and *S.O.B.*, which was loosely based on your experiences making *Darling Lili*. The Preston Sturges Award you're getting seems especially appropriate because the fiascos, in retrospect, would fit wickedly into a Sturges satire.

Edwards: The big ones were *Darling Lili* at Paramount and *Wild Rovers* at MGM. I was wounded badly by *Darling Lili*. Then there was *The Carey Treatment*, which I did because I was led to believe that the film would make up for all the studio interference I had faced on *Wild Rovers*. The stories on *Carey Treatment* make me sick—lies and deceit to the point where I finished the film and never cut it. I just handed it over to Ralph Winters and said, "I'm through, Ralph."

And Julie [Andrews] kept saying, "You'll be back." So, I thought, I will write my own screenplay. It will never be seen. It was the kind of subject I liked to do in radio and television—a private-eye picture. It was purely creative—just to let the wounds heal. Then I put it away, and I finally took it off the shelf. This became *City Heat*. Everything that happened on that picture just destroyed me. I really don't know what Hollywood is. It certainly isn't geographic for me. There's a corruptness about it that I resist. It's not that I'm a saint or that I never fucked up or that I didn't do corrupt things myself—I did. But I'm not comfortable with that. I fought it every time. And I resist it now.

Roberts: Looking back, what are the dream projects that got away?
Edwards: A lot. I bought a book by Saul Bellow that I just love. But it's difficult to do. It's *Henderson the Rain King*. And I just can't cast it. Plus there's the ongoing struggle for me of being—in others' eyes—not the right director for that sort of piece. I also had a project about the battle of Gettysburg. It was told from the viewpoint of the people in the town. This thing just descended on them, this enormous battle, and the movie shows how they reacted and what effect it had on them.

Also, I've just finished a screenplay that's very autobiographical. I know I can sell it, but I don't know if I'll be let to direct it. It's about horrendous domestic problems. My wife and I each went through having parents die. It deals with problems with our kids. Things were very tough. Leo McCarey once told me that there's a point you reach in your personal problems that he called "breaking the pain barrier." One night in the midst of all of this, I started to laugh. And I laughed and laughed. Once I got beyond the tragic aspect, past the point where I finally could have some objectivity, past that pain barrier that McCarey was talking about, I let it out. The script is called *It Never Rains*.

Roberts: You started out as an actor. How has your acting experience helped you as a director?
Edwards: Enormously. I understand what an actor is feeling and going through. Today when I write, I act it in my head. As a former actor you have a rapport with the cast. It's like convicts with other convicts: You all understand what this is. I start a scene by saying, "Show me." I don't direct, actually. I try to hire the best actors. Then I let them do what they do best. After a rehearsal or run-through, then I might help stage what they do a little bit so that the camera gets it all.

Roberts: Many people remember comedy set pieces from your films. I love the scene in *The Man Who Loved Women* where Burt Reynolds is trying to keep quiet in the closet and gets that frou-frou dog glued to his hand.
Edwards: I was always pleased with the dog-stuck-to-the-hand scene. There are certain sequences out of the *Panthers* that I like. There are a couple in *10*. So much of those things are happenings out of my life. My family is accident prone. I've got an accident-prone gene. I'm convinced of that. My daughter spills everything all the time. Got it from me. The Clouseau gene.

We moved into a new house with new furniture and a beautiful carpet. Three different nights—not consecutive nights, but close together—she spilled chocolate yogurt. There's always a mad scramble to clean it up. Julie runs into the kitchen and so forth. They're soaking it up. So it was decided that she wasn't going to bring it in anymore. Ok, fine. Then one night I brought my dish in. Then my daughter comes in, tripped and hit into me, and the goddamn chocolate goes everywhere. So sometimes you don't need to create.

Blake Edwards: In the Pink

Bill Desowitz / 1999

From *Los Angeles Times*, November 4, 1999, pp. 16–17, 18. Reprinted by permission of Bill Desowitz.

Like his bumbling screen detective, Inspector Clouseau, Blake Edwards is a survivor. The seventy-seven-year-old filmmaker has covered a lot of territory, from the sublime *Breakfast at Tiffany's* (1961) to the outrageous *S.O.B.* (1981). Although he will forever be associated with the commercially successful *Pink Panther* film series and *10* (1979), his artistic triumph remains the uproarious and elegant *Victor/Victoria* (1982). Yet the full measure of his talent can be found in such overlooked films as *Darling Lili* (1970), *Experiment in Terror* (1962), and *Wild Rovers* (1971), which explore the depths of human frailty with compassion and sometimes absurdity.

Unpredictability is everything in an Edwards film. Just when you think things can't get any worse, they usually do, and in the most hysterical and humiliating ways. As if to illustrate the point, a lens accidentally pops out of the frame while he plays with his glasses during a recent interview in his penthouse office. "I am Clouseau," he quips. "It's the story of my life."

However, the resilient director launched his film career at just the right time, when an exciting, new, and independent Hollywood overtook the old studio system in the sixties. Edwards worked at the height of the feminist and sexual revolutions, and it shows in his diverse films, in which love and marriage and the male ego take quite a pounding. Then again, you come away from an Edwards film with the firm belief that nothing can be taken for granted, so you had better toughen up.

Friday through November 27, Edwards will be the subject of a film tribute at the Los Angeles County Museum of Art. He will appear in person November 13 with a screening of *S.O.B.*, his vicious attack on the Hollywood power brokers who some would say have bottom-lined creativity out of the industry. Seeing him today, in preproduction on *It Never Rains*, an independently produced film to star Chevy

Chase as a struggling writer, you immediately sense that he's lost the spring in his step but none of his vital sense of humor.

Bill Desowitz: Whatever genre you've explored, there's always a provocative and even subversive exploration of love and sexual identity. Did you run into many problems getting this subject matter on screen?

Blake Edwards: Many times. It took me six years to get *10* made. And then I literally had to blackmail the company by saying I would do another *Panther* for them. I didn't, but it paid off.

BD: Even *The Pink Panther* series undermines male dominance in a very farcical way.

BE: I'll take your word for it. I don't analyze my films like that. I have enough trouble analyzing my life. I like that kind of robust humor. Most critics like to call it slapstick, but they don't know the first thing about slapstick. I feel like one of the early barnstorming pilots that flew by the seat of their pants—there were a lot of things that affected me, made up my view of humor and comedy. The old-timers when I was young like Laurel and Hardy—I was fortunate when I was very young in my craft to be involved with filmmakers who would do that kind of humor. And I learned almost by osmosis. You couldn't help finding yourself really laughing from the gut, being interested in why that takes the blues away.

BD: You could say *Breakfast at Tiffany's* is about taking the blues away. Did Audrey Hepburn surprise you in any way?

BE: No, not really. I was in love with her before that movie. I wasn't surprised, except by her sense of humor. She certainly showed great enthusiasm. But she was that way in anything she did. I think she did more for me.

BD: As did [film composer] Henry Mancini. How did you two meet?

BE: As it's happened so much in my life, there was a kind of serendipity. I was just getting a break at Universal, and I felt a show needed a love theme. They asked me to come over and listen to something. I thought, "Jesus, this is really good. Where did you get that?" And they introduced me to Hank. I was walking into the commissary, and he was coming out. I yelled, "Hey, Hank." And he said, "Hi, coach." I said, "You wanna do a television show?" He said, "Sure." I sent him over the script, and he read it and asked if he could do jazz. I told him he could do anything he liked. And that was the beginning of *Peter Gunn*.

BD: And Julie Andrews?

BE: I had an idea for a script dealing with a Mata Hari, a female spy, who was an

BILL DESOWITZ / 1999   **111**

entertainer [*Darling Lili*]. I made an appointment with her agent, and I went up to her house—and that was it. It just kind of happened. She wanted me to stay for dinner, and I couldn't. I didn't call for two weeks, and she said, "Well, that was a real bust." And I was sick. I was really suffering. And then I did call, and we started seeing each other. Nothing terribly unusual about it; we just fell in love.

BD: And you've been married for thirty years. Although *Darling Lili* was a notorious box office failure and the inspiration for *S.O.B.*, it may be your richest film. It's every Blake Edwards film rolled into one.
BE: You know, films like that drive me crazy because I think that I'm objective enough to know even when I'm not being objective. There's so much good stuff in that film. There were two big problems that I passionately fought. From the very beginning, I told Paramount they were nuts for wanting to shoot on location in Ireland. Because this is not an easy film to do, and you're making it [ten] times more difficult with the [expletive] weather. Not only that, we were so preoccupied with the aerial photography, and they insisted I use every bit of it. Plus, as we went along, I began to see that the degree of the musical numbers threw the whole thing off pace. So it wasn't the film that I truly wanted to make, but I thought it was a good film.

BD: The other great collaboration, of course, was with Peter Sellers.
BE: That was a fluke too. Peter Ustinov backed out of *The Pink Panther* after we couldn't deliver Ava Gardner. I was desperate to make this film, so I took a chance with Peter. I met him in Rome, and we drove from the airport to the hotel. By the time we got to the hotel, we found out that in very important respects we were soulmates—that we both adored Laurel and Hardy and [Buster] Keaton and you name it. We were testing each other to see who knew the most. And he really knew a lot. He said, "Well, can we do that with this character?" And I said, "Absolutely, you bet." And that was the beginning. He was a total schizophrenic. One film he was sensational; the next film he was a horror—you know, calling me up in the middle of the night and telling me he just spoke with God, who told him how to do the scene. I told him: "Tell God to stay out of show business."

Interview with Blake Edwards

Larry King / 2002

From CNN *Larry King Weekend*, July 27, 2002. Reprinted by permission of CNN.

[Ed. Note: This interview was part of a larger program, including a separate interview with Jack Valenti, a debate with experts on nuclear policy, and entertainment by Josh Groban. Clips from Edwards's films were played during his interview.]

LARRY KING: Tonight, can Hollywood make 10 again? Famed writer-director Blake Edwards, who's also Julie Andrews's husband, aims to find out.

How do America's presidents stack up as speech makers? Jack Valenti, president of the Motion Picture Association and former aide to LBJ hands out grades and tells us how to speak up with confidence; and then an explosive discussion on US nuclear policy—a recipe for national defense or global disaster?

Squaring off, world-renowned antinuclear activist Dr. Helen Caldicott, a Nobel Peace Prize nominee, and Frank Gaffney, Pentagon official under Ronald Reagan and now president of the Center for Security Policy.

And then a song from rising music superstar Josh Groban, all next on *Larry King Weekend*.

Jack Valenti joins us later. Our first guest tonight—what a great pleasure to finally have him here—Blake Edwards, writer, director, producer of films, television, stage, what a career, a rollercoaster career that keeps on keeping on. Blake Edwards, a long successful marriage with Julie Andrews. Are you doing 10 over?

BLAKE EDWARDS: Yes.

KING: Explain. It's called "10 Again"?

EDWARDS: "10 Again."

KING: Explain that to me.

EDWARDS: Well, it's a long story of how I got involved in it. An actor who is obsessed by it, a young actor as a matter of fact—I met with him. He told me how much he loved it. He pushed the button, I guess, and it made me say, you know, that was twenty-some years ago.

KING: Dudley and Bo.
EDWARDS: That's right, and I thought, I had such a good time and it was so much fun that I'd try it again.

KING: And what did Julie think?
EDWARDS: Oh, she just said, "That's nice, dear."

KING: Did she enjoy it, too?
EDWARDS: Making the original, you mean?

KING: Yes.
EDWARDS: Oh, yes, she loved it.

KING: Are you just going to make it again with a new cast and just do it over?
EDWARDS: Well, not quite that. Instead of being two songwriters in California, it's two songwriters in New York—more like Lerner and Lowe, theater background, that sort of thing—instead of going into Mexico and the sun and the hot beaches, they'll go into the snow.

KING: Will they see her?
EDWARDS: What?

KING: The snow?
EDWARDS: Oh, yes, so we'll have fun in the snow.

KING: So she comes walking out of a snowstorm?
EDWARDS: Well, not a bad idea. Yes, why not.

KING: Would you say, Blake, it's fair to say that one of the things about your greatness—and you have the French Legion of Honor on your jacket which says a lot about your greatness—was that you were always a risk taker?
EDWARDS: I've been told that. I think I am.

KING: You're not conventional.
EDWARDS: No.

KING: How did you start?

EDWARDS: Well, I started, you know, as a kid that came out from Oklahoma. My parents were out here. I was born in Oklahoma, and when I was old enough I came out here. My stepfather at that time was in the film business, and, as a matter of fact, we lived practically on the back lot of Fox, right in that area in Beverly Hills. And, it was that or be a thief, I guess.

KING: So you grew up with this?

EDWARDS: Grew up in the business, yes.

KING: What was the—and you were an assistant director?

EDWARDS: No, I was an actor to begin with and then along came World War whatever it was.

KING: It was in all the papers.

EDWARDS: Was it World War II that was in the paper? I can't remember. I hate to tell you what I did in World War II, but anyway along that came so it stopped everything for a while. Then I came back, and I thought, well, it's an easy life. It's fun, but I just wasn't satisfied with it and eventually things happened. Serendipity occurred, which is part of my life. I started writing for radio and then from radio I went into television and television into films.

KING: What was your first movie?

EDWARDS: First that I?

KING: Directed.

EDWARDS: Oh, that I directed. The first movie that I directed was a thing with Frankie Laine called *Bring Your Smile Along*. Yes, and it started out like twelve-day musicals.

KING: What was the first hit?

EDWARDS: The first hit?

KING: How did America get to know the name Blake Edwards?

EDWARDS: I think probably because of the importance, I guess that would be the word, of *Breakfast at Tiffany's*. I think probably that was the first big thing where everybody said, "Whoops, who is he?"

KING: How did you get that gig? That was an amazing picture.

EDWARDS: Well, it was by attrition. I started doing inexpensive little films at

Columbia, and people thought I was talented. So I went over to Universal, and I did films that were a little more expensive. Eventually, I guess the segue, the bridge, was probably a film that I did with Cary Grant called *Operation Petticoat*.

KING: Not a bad film.
EDWARDS: No, not a bad film at all.

KING: Tony Curtis, too, right?
EDWARDS: Yes, and so from there I started to climb the hill.

KING: Did you know when you had *Breakfast at Tiffany's* done that it was special?
EDWARDS: No. I knew it was special because of her [Audrey Hepburn]. She was a wonderful, wonderful person. It was great fun and all of that stuff, but I didn't like it that much when it was done. I wasn't that much in love with it. There was a lot that I would have done that . . .

KING: Over again? You'd have done it differently if you had to do it over?
EDWARDS: Yes.

KING: Really?
EDWARDS: Yes. Well, I would have stuck more with the Capote book. It was tougher. When I came into it, they were talking about [Marilyn] Monroe doing the lead and not Audrey, so that's a whole different character.

KING: Yes.
EDWARDS: A lady that gets $50 for going to the powder room and stuff like that.

KING: Did you like George Peppard?
EDWARDS: Did I like him? Yes, I liked George.

KING: Good guy.
EDWARDS: He drove me crazy, but I loved him. He was just great, and he was very decent with me.

KING: Died too young.
EDWARDS: Yes, he did.

KING: How did you meet Julie Andrews?
EDWARDS: Crossing Sunset Boulevard. For about six mornings I was going across Sunset. You know they used to have a bridle path on Sunset. You would cross

Sunset and stop on that bridle path while the cars passed, and then you'd go on. I kept ending up in this island with Julie Andrews, and I kept looking over. I finally said, "Are you coming from where I'm going or the opposite of that?" She said, "I think so," and it turned out we were both going to our analyst or coming from our analyst, two coincidental precise . . .

KING: She was a star then, right?
EDWARDS: Yes. Yes, she was.

KING: *My Fair Lady* and . . .
EDWARDS: I had met her at a party or something like that.

KING: Had she done *Mary Poppins* already?
EDWARDS: Yes. Yes. She was well established by that time. I wouldn't have stopped if she hadn't been well established.

KING: And when you got married, you worked together?
EDWARDS: Yes.

KING: Was that difficult or easy?
EDWARDS: It was very easy, as a matter of fact. We agreed on two things when we got married. We'd take it a day at a time, and we'd work together whenever we could so that we spent enough time together. We didn't think it was going to last, so we might as well have a good time.

KING: How long are you married now?
EDWARDS: It will be thirty-five years soon.

KING: And what a lady.
EDWARDS: Yes.

KING: How's she doing, by the way? I know there's—I don't want to get into the lawsuits and everything.
EDWARDS: She's doing magnificently. That's all I can say. It would be hard for her not to. She's a very unique person, a very brave person and . . .

KING: But she can't sing, right?
EDWARDS: No. She's finished.

KING: What a tragedy.
EDWARDS: Tragic.

KING: She can still act though, right?
EDWARDS: Oh, yes, and she's got a big children's book business. She and her daughter [Emma Walton] write children's books, and they got a publishing company. Oh they're—she's in New York now, and you know she's busy.

KING: Blake Edwards. Still to come, a musical based on the *Pink Panther*. We have got to talk about the *Pink Panther*. What a career. What a guy. We'll be right back.

[Video clips from *Breakfast at Tiffany's* and *Victor/Victoria*]

KING: Now *Victor/Victoria*—Blake Edwards is our guest—did you bring that to the stage?
EDWARDS: Yes.

KING: You did the movie, too, right?
EDWARDS: Yes.

KING: And you got the idea to do a musical?
EDWARDS: Yes.

KING: Now, I loved that show, saw it twice. It got mixed reviews.
EDWARDS: Yes.

KING: Looking back, why?
EDWARDS: Well, I don't want to throw a lot of sour grapes, but . . .

KING: Go ahead.
EDWARDS: OK. Because I was an upstart from . . .

KING: You weren't a Broadway guy?
EDWARDS: No. I'm sure that's it.

KING: You're one of those movie guys coming here telling us how to do a show?
EDWARDS: That's right, and there's no doubt in my mind that that was the main part of it.

KING: Because it was a wonderful show.

EDWARDS: Oh, well, if you went there, you saw it—every night a standing ovation.

KING: Every night.

EDWARDS: Every night jammed to the rafters.

KING: And Julie refused her Tony nomination.

EDWARDS: We didn't get one nomination.

KING: Except her, right?

EDWARDS: Except her. You know the sets, the choreography, things like that didn't—it could only have been . . .

KING: Have you revived it with someone else doing it?

EDWARDS: It has been done in various places. I understand it's going to have a revival. It's going to open I think in Paris.

KING: The movie was fantastic.

EDWARDS: Yes, wasn't it?

KING: What was it like to work with Robert Preston? You did a few things with him.

EDWARDS: He was such a mensch. That's the only way I can describe him. You know I called him up, and I said, "Pres," we'd already done *S.O.B.*

KING: Oh, what a movie.

EDWARDS: And I said, "I want you to do a film." He said, "OK." I said, "You're going to play gay," and he said, "OK." I said, "Do you understand what I just said? I want you to"—because playing gay at that time was not the simplest transition in the world.

KING: Many would have turned it down.

EDWARDS: Sure, many did, you know, two or three very important men turned it down, not just that part, but turned down the other part because it had to do with homosexuality and show biz and stuff like that.

KING: He played gay great, though, didn't he?

EDWARDS: Oh, didn't he? Because he didn't play gay, you know.

KING: Yes, that's right, he played it.
EDWARDS: Yes, that's right.

KING: And Garner, James Garner was . . .
EDWARDS: Oh, well. See Jimbo is for me the best reactor in the business. That's what's great about him. Nobody reacts better than Garner. I mean, you . . .

KING: Underrated in a sense. When they talk about great, you don't think about him.
EDWARDS: Yes, I think so. Sure. No. No. You don't think of him in terms of greatness and things like that, but in those terms you can't top him. There's nobody that can react to something like Jim can.

KING: Tell me about Blake Edwards and the *Pink Panther*.
EDWARDS: Well, the *Pink Panther*, bless his greedy little heart, has provided me with a comfortable life.

KING: I would say.
EDWARDS: And . . .

KING: How many of them did you do?
EDWARDS: Gee, I think six or seven, maybe eight.

KING: One without Sellers, right?
EDWARDS: Oh, we did two without Sellers.

KING: One with?
EDWARDS: I don't remember anymore, but yes, I think it was two without Sellers, after Sellers had passed on.

KING: Yes.
EDWARDS: And we're going to do a musical. We've got a book. We've got a score. It looks like we got the money.

KING: Do you have the lead?
EDWARDS: No. No, but we've got some ideas.

KING: What was Sellers's genius?
EDWARDS: It's hard to tell. It's hard to say. I've gone to that well so many times trying to figure it out. He was crazy, and I . . .

KING: He was off-screen crazy.

EDWARDS: Yes, and out of his craziness in some way blossomed this genius for being able to step aside from himself and see the—I can remember times when he would be in the middle of a scene, and he would break up. He would start giggling, and I would say, "God, what is going on?" He'd say, "Can you imagine this? Look at this idiot," and he would talk about his idiot.

KING: Like it was someone else?

EDWARDS: Yes, and it was someone else for Sellers.

KING: Did you laugh on the set when he would do this?

EDWARDS: Oh, terribly. Sometimes, and, I mean this, I'm not just offering. If you want to have the best time you've ever had, give me a call, and I'll run you the outtakes. They are to die over. They really are. That's the best entertainment you'll ever have.

KING: Was he difficult?

EDWARDS: Yes, terrible.

KING: I've heard that. They didn't like him.

EDWARDS: Just, well, because he was crazy.

KING: It was hard to like him?

EDWARDS: Oh, you couldn't like him. You couldn't really like him. You might feel sorry for him. You might like something he's done, but to truly like the man—he was not a likable man. He was—there were times when it almost bordered on evil.

KING: Did you expect the movies to do as well as they did?

EDWARDS: No. No, absolutely not. After, like, the third, we expected that they probably would because they had been doing well, and there was every reason to believe that they would continue to do so.

KING: Who cast that wonderful Herbert Lom, the head of detectives that would always drive him nuts and send him to an insane asylum?

EDWARDS: You know, I sort of inherited a lot of those people because they were part of the English film industry and part of Sellers . . .

KING: His group?

EDWARDS: Yes, I think Lom did *I'm All Right, Jack* or one of those with Sellers.

KING: He was great.
EDWARDS: Oh, yes.

KING: Funny.
EDWARDS: Oh, yes, they were terrific.

KING: Did you have fun doing them even though you didn't like the lead guy?
EDWARDS: Best time I ever had. It's the only thing that had me coming back.

KING: Did you hire Mancini to do the music?
EDWARDS: Yes, sure.

KING: Because of *Tiffany's*?
EDWARDS: No, because of—it goes all the way back to radio—I mean, to television. I was doing a film. Hank came in to write one piece of music that I wanted written. I never met him before. I saw him a few days later at their commissary and said, "My life is so full of serendipity, of things happening like this. I want to do a television show." He said, "Sure, what is it?" I said, "I'm calling it *Peter Gunn*." And he said, "OK, yes." I said, "I'll send you the script." He thought it was going to be a western, and he called me up and said . . .

KING: One of the great television themes ever written.
EDWARDS: Yes, and he said, "Can I do a jazz score?" I said, "You can do anything you want. I love jazz." I grew up with jazz, and it really appealed to me. The first piece of music that I heard was that theme when he called me up, asked me over to the stage, and what is that expression, [inaudible]? I [inaudible] all over the stage.

KING: Our guest is the great Blake Edwards. We'll be back with some more and then Jack Valenti. This will be the first of other visits, I hope, with a genius. Don't go away.

[Video clip from *The Pink Panther*]

KING: You did *Days of Wine and Roses*, with Jack Lemmon—wonderful movie. Were you an alcoholic, or did you have depression or both?
EDWARDS: Well, both, but I am an alcoholic.

KING: Did one lead to the other?
EDWARDS: It's kind of hard to say. They kind of go hand in hand, at least they did with me.

KING: Were you drinking when you made that movie?

EDWARDS: Yes, both of us were drinking.

KING: You and Lemmon?

EDWARDS: Yes. We got together for dinner afterwards, and I said, "Jack, did it bother you that we're doing this movie, and we're living these roles?" And he said, "It didn't bother me particularly." I went on talking about it. I said, "You know, I'm so disturbed now. I can't enjoy myself drinking." He said, "Well, I don't have that problem yet." Finally we talked about it, and I realized he was giving me back lines out of the script. I pointed it out to him. I said, "You're giving me the character phrase." Well, OK. And he said, "Are you really disturbed by that?" I said, "I really am." He said, "Are you going to stop drinking because of it?" I said, "No," and he said, "Well, neither am I," and we went on drinking.

KING: How did you stop?

EDWARDS: I stopped—it was a matter of a lot of things. I was injured in the service, which we won't go into. It's a story all unto itself.

KING: Next time.

EDWARDS: OK. I became hooked on drugs, so it was drugs and booze and a whole compulsive lifestyle. As a writer I was smoking two, three packs of cigarettes a day, and one day I just said, "That's it. I can't handle it anymore." I stopped drinking and I stopped smoking, and I practically stopped breathing, but . . .

KING: Cut them out both at the same time?

EDWARDS: Yes, all of it.

KING: How long sober?

EDWARDS: God, nearly forty years.

KING: Do you do AA or anything like that?

EDWARDS: I did somewhat in the beginning, but it's interesting because I was struggling with cigarettes. I was struggling with morphine. I was struggling with all of this.

KING: All of the above.

EDWARDS: Yes. So it was—thank God I had a career that was taking off. I know some people aren't lucky enough to be able to seize that opportunity. I was so desperate to succeed and be something that I was driven.

KING: The goal was greater than the . . .
EDWARDS: Yes, that's exactly right.

KING: How about the depression, how did you . . .
EDWARDS: Terrible, just . . .

KING: Into your success?
EDWARDS: Oh, yes. My depression has been with me most of my life that I can remember. I have spells of it.

KING: Still?
EDWARDS: Yes, still. I haven't for quite a while.

KING: Do you take medication?
EDWARDS: I'm not on it now. I was.

KING: Did Julie help?
EDWARDS: Oh, yes. I don't think I could have gotten—that sounds melodramatic, but I really don't think I could have gotten through without her.

KING: It is clinical, right? I mean, they . . .
EDWARDS: Yes.

KING: Someone would look at you and say, "Hey, there's no reason for you to be depressed."
EDWARDS: No, it's clinical.

KING: So it's not explainable?
EDWARDS: No. It has nothing to do with lifestyle and things like that.

KING: Did you ever think of harming yourself?
EDWARDS: Excuse me?

KING: Ever think of harming yourself?
EDWARDS: Yes. In fact, I can tell you some very funny stories about that.

KING: Tell me one.
EDWARDS: OK. I had decided that the time had come. I didn't want to live anymore. I went up on a bluff in Malibu where we lived. I had decided on the method,

which was probably to slash my wrists because I figured I could bleed into the lawn and nobody would notice it. I got a straight razor blade, and I sat down in a chair on a beautiful sunny day looking out at the Pacific. I'm in my tennis shorts, and as I prepared to do the deed, I felt a wet nose at my ear. I responded. It was my Great Dane, and he knew something was going on. He just knew, and I said, "Get away. Go away." I pushed him away, and finally he became so almost-abusive trying to get me to stop doing whatever it was I was doing. I had locked him up in my studio, but I could see him through the glass because it was an all-glass studio.

KING: He knew?

EDWARDS: Yes, he knew. He was jumping and running and whining. You could hear him. And I thought, well, in a little while that won't make any difference. I won't have to worry about him, and I'm ready to do it again. And I feel this wet, soggy thing at my crotch, and I look down. It's a tennis ball and our other dog, our retriever, had now brought me a tennis ball. He knew what the hell was going on, and he kept fetching this tennis ball. I kept saying, "Go away," and throwing the tennis ball.

KING: This is the suicide gone wrong.

EDWARDS: Right. So finally, I figured, I know what I'll do. I'll throw this ball over the cliff. It will go down on the beach. By the time he finds it and retrieves it . . .

KING: You're dead.

EDWARDS: I'm dead, right? So I wind up and throw the tennis ball, and I dislocate my shoulder. I fall over backwards in the chair, and I decided at that moment that today was not the day for it.

KING: The gang that couldn't shoot straight.

EDWARDS: So I turned around and started back toward the house feeling just terrible, and I thought, oh, wait a minute. You know, always the one to worry about other people and I thought that razor blade's in the lawn somewhere. So I went over looking for the razor blade and stepped on it and cut open my heel up about that deep and ended up in the emergency in Malibu saying, "Hurry up, or I'm going to bleed to death." That was one suicide attempt.

KING: What a great—that's incredible.

EDWARDS: Yes, it's true.

KING: Taught you a lesson, though. You believe the dogs knew, though?

EDWARDS: Oh, they knew. There's no doubt they knew. Absolutely.

KING: Blake, I want many more visits with you. You're an intriguing person whom I've admired for years.
EDWARDS: Thank you.

KING: And we looked forward to this, and I look forward to it again.
EDWARDS: Thank you, Larry.

KING: And we look forward to *10 Again*.
EDWARDS: Good.

KING: And the musical of the *Pink Panther*.
EDWARDS: Yes.

KING: The one, the only, Blake Edwards. He'll be back. Jack Valenti, another of my favorite people is next. Don't go away.

An Active Imagination

Susan King / 2003

From *Los Angeles Times*, December 25, 2003. Reprinted by permission of *Los Angeles Times*.

Eyeing the blond in the next booth at the Polo Lounge as she stands up to leave, Blake Edwards jokes that there was a reason he wrote and directed the comedy *10*.

His blue eyes twinkle as he watches the statuesque twentysomething put on her raincoat—it's the same type of look Dudley Moore gave Bo Derek the first time he caught a glimpse of her in the 1979 hit that Edwards wrote and directed. Never mind that the woman is casting off vibes that she knows she's attractive.

"I don't have to know that," he says with a smile. "I can sit back here and imagine her. I can imagine you, whoever you are, kiddo. So you have been imagined and taken in."

Edwards is now eighty-one. For the last twenty years, he's suffered from the disease commonly known by the misnomer *chronic fatigue syndrome*.

But he's quick to point out that he directed numerous movies during that time and even directed wife Julie Andrews on Broadway a decade or so ago in the theatrical version of his 1982 movie musical hit, *Victor/Victoria*.

Though he hasn't directed a film since 1993's *Son of the Pink Panther*, Edwards is constantly at work, spending most of his nights writing. "How many things did I write last year? Three plays and two screenplays."

He also did the poignant audio commentary track for the upcoming DVD of *The Days of Wine and Roses*, the acclaimed 1962 drama about a young couple's (Jack Lemmon and Lee Remick) battle with alcoholism. The Warner Home Video disc arrives in stores January 6.

Just a few hours before this interview, the Academy of Motion Picture Arts and Science announced that its board of governors had selected Edwards to receive an honorary Oscar February 29 for "extraordinary distinction in lifetime achievement." The citation on the award will read: "In recognition of his writing, directing, and producing an extraordinary body of work for the screen."

"I would be lying to you if [I said] I wasn't flattered by it," he says. "I would be lying about it if [I said] it didn't keep me up all night. I kept drifting away from what I was doing, thinking about my past and how I got here."

Although he's made such classics as *Operation Mad Ball*, *Breakfast at Tiffany's*, the *Pink Panther* comedies, *The Party*, *10*, *S.O.B.*, and *Victor/Victoria*, Edwards's only Oscar nomination has been for the screenplay adaptation of *Victor/Victoria*. He's won awards from the Writers Guild, received a Golden Globe nomination, and other honors and awards here and abroad, but the movie academy has all but ignored him.

"I have to tell you, I never thought I was going to get an Oscar," he says matter-of-factly. "I felt like there were times when I should have been nominated. I was very philosophical about it. If it didn't happen, it didn't happen. I have had awards, and I have had a hell of a life. I can't do much better. So this is gravy. It's wonderful."

Beginning Friday, the American Cinematheque at the Egyptian Theatre in Holly-wood is paying tribute to Edwards with a retrospective of the *Pink Panther* comedies he made with Peter Sellers from 1964 to 1978: *The Pink Panther*, *A Shot in the Dark*, *The Return of the Pink Panther*, *The Pink Panther Strikes Again*, and *Revenge of the Pink Panther*.

Set to Henry Mancini's melodious scores, the *Pink Panther* comedies are filled with silly puns and sight gags that the giants of silent screen comedy would have envied. Even four decades after the first two *Panther* films were made, the movies remain remarkably fresh and funny, and Sellers's disaster-prone French police officer, Inspector Clouseau, is one of cinema's great comedic creations.

"I'm flattered," says Edwards, "anytime they feel something I did was good enough to do a retrospective. . . . But on the other hand, and people are going to say this is sour grapes—and that's all right because I have been a critic of the industry all of my adult life—but they are going to remake the *Panther* and they are going to remake *The Party* and nobody, no one has talked to me about it.

"Home Box Office just did *The Life and Death of Peter Sellers*, and there is not one word of truth in it," Edwards continues. "I had seen [the first draft of the script], and I saw it only by my request. I said, 'I hear you are doing this. I am surprised. Where are you getting your information?' They are not even taking it from the book [about Sellers]. I thought the actor who plays me [John Lithgow] might think that maybe I have something I could tell him. I have stories. . . . "

But what really puzzles Edwards is why Steve Martin would want to be the new Clouseau. Edwards attempted to make two Clouseau comedies after the death of Sellers with Ted Wass and Roberto Benigni; both failed.

"He doesn't have to prove anything, even to himself," says Edwards of Martin. "Why put himself in competition with Sellers? He's not even going to come close to Sellers. He may do something great on his own. That I don't know. He is not going to be Clouseau."

Proust Questionnaire: Blake Edwards

Vanity Fair / 2004

The onetime boy auteur who reinvented the American movie comedy and perfected the genre of the sophisticated sixties CinemaScope farce, Blake Edwards has had many high-water marks in his sixty-two-year career, directing films such as *Breakfast at Tiffany's*, *The Great Race*, and *Victor/Victoria* (starring wife Julie Andrews). This month, forty years after the release of his original *Pink Panther*, the Academy is honoring him on Oscar night with its lifetime-achievement award.

Vanity Fair: What is your idea of perfect happiness?
Blake Edwards: Listening to Renata Tebaldi sing Puccini's "Un bel di."

VF: What is your greatest fear?
BE: Losing my hearing.

VF: Which living person do you most admire?
BE: My wife.

VF: What is the trait you most deplore in yourself?
BE: Arrogance.

VF: What is your greatest extravagance?
BE: Buying expensive things to make it look like I'm richer than I am.

VF: On what occasion do you lie?
BE: Whenever I think it's going to do me more good than telling the truth.

VF: Which living person do you most despise?
BE: I don't despise. Anything beyond "pissed off" is a waste of time and energy.

VF: What or who is the greatest love of your life?
BE: Julie and Henry.

VF: When and where were you happiest?
BE: Ever since Julie and I got married and Henry the cat took up residence.

VF: Which talent would you most like to have?
BE: I'd give my soul to be a great tenor.

VF: What do you consider your greatest achievement?
BE: My family and a certain amount of success in my chosen fields of endeavor.

VF: What do you regard as the lowest depth of misery?
BE: To lose one's sense of humor.

VF: Where would you like to live?
BE: Comfortably in myself.

VF: What is your favorite occupation?
BE: Pretending.

VF: What do you most value in your friends?
BE: Loyalty.

VF: What is your favorite hero of fiction?
BE: Tarzan and Cheetah.

VF: Who are your heroes in real life?
BE: Wyatt Earp and Doc Holliday.

VF: What is it that you most dislike?
BE: Compromise when you know you shouldn't.

VF: How would you like to die?
BE: Slaying dragons.

VF: What is your motto?
BE: The 11th Commandment as set forth to me by Gene Fowler on his deathbed: "Thou shalt not give up."

The Art of Blake Edwards at the Pacific Design Center

David Ng / 2009

From *Los Angeles Times*, January 18, 2009. Reprinted by permission of *Los Angeles Times*.

Blake Edwards remembers shopping for sculptures to be featured in *The Man Who Loved Women*, his 1983 comedy that starred Burt Reynolds as an artist who spends more time in the bedroom than in the studio. But the director was having difficulty finding the kind of abstract art that he thought the film needed.

"I wanted the sculptures to be all original works since this was a movie about an artist," Edwards recalls. At the insistence of friends, the director, an amateur artist himself, decided to take on the challenge of creating the sculptures for his own movie, one of which was a large-scale outdoor installation composed of swooping curves that he eventually titled *Man of the World*.

Though the movie has long since faded from memory, *Man of the World* lives on and can be seen in a smaller-scaled bronze version in *The Art of Blake Edwards*, a retrospective of the director's work at the Pacific Design Center through January 30.

The show represents the first time in twenty-five years that Edwards's art has been shown in public.

"I didn't want to do it," Edwards says of the exhibition. "My artwork is my own private vice—I don't have to worry about competing with anyone or worrying what the critics would say. Even by giving this interview, I feel like I've sold out to the devil."

Eventually, Edwards's family, including his wife, Julie Andrews, persuaded him to go forward with the show. The exhibition contains close to 130 paintings and sculptures.

"The works are very diverse, but you see the same sense of humor and whimsy as in his films," says Gail Oppenheimer, the curator of the show.

Edwards, best known for *10*, *Victor/Victoria*, and the *Pink Panther* films, started creating art in 1969 and has completed more than two hundred works. His paintings fall mostly within the Abstract Expressionist category, with bright colors and Surrealistic touches that suggest the influences of Joan Miro, Paul Klee, and Pablo Picasso.

One recurring image in the exhibition is a duck. Several bronze sculptures feature the birds in comic repose, sitting on their tail feathers. "I'm sure it has to do with the time I gave an interview, and I was asked, in effect, what I do about critics who don't like my films," recounts Edwards. "So I said to them, 'I just duck.'

"The exhibition also features jewelry that the director made for his wife. "I was traveling, and I told him that I wished I could take something that was his," Andrews recalls. "And that was the beginning of that."

Though he is now eighty-six, Edwards says he has no plans to stop working on his art. "I may have stopped making films, but I'm not going to stop making paintings and sculptures."

Old School

David Mermelstein / 2009

From *DGA Quarterly*, Summer 2009 issue. Reprinted courtesy of the Directors Guild of America, Inc.

Inspired by the silent clowns, Blake Edwards created the *Pink Panther* franchise and some of the craftiest comedies to come out of Hollywood. But sight gags, mistaken identities, and flying pies were not all he had in his bag of tricks.

Blake Edwards's classic comedies have always had a dark side, so it's not surprising the director best known for his series of *Pink Panther* films has mixed feelings about being celebrated solely as a master of the pratfall.

"It gets a little tiresome," he admitted recently, sitting in the light-filled living room of his Brentwood home. "I have made other things. I don't mind being the comedy maven." He pauses. "But I do, I guess." And yet here he was—closing in on eighty-seven, his memory razor-sharp—expounding on the art of comedy by recalling not just some of the more celebrated scenes in his oeuvre, but also how it was that he, um, stumbled into such fare to begin with.

Edwards insists he never embarked on a career as a comedy director. It just sort of happened. "I learned a long time ago," he says, "that if I have a talent for directing comedy, it's best not to question it. Do it." He will forever be associated with the eight *Pink Panther* movies he made between 1963 and 1993, especially the five starring Peter Sellers as the bumbling Inspector Clouseau. It was a fruitful if complicated relationship.

"We clicked on comedy," Edwards says, "and we were lucky we found each other because we both had so much respect for it. We also had an ability to come up with funny things and great situations that had to be explored. But in that exploration there would oftentimes be disagreement. . . . But I couldn't resist those moments when we jelled. And if you ask me who contributed most to those things, it couldn't have happened unless both of us were involved, even though it wasn't always happy."

The director maintains that Clouseau's appeal, then and now, lies in his per-
severance. "Thou shalt not give up," says Edwards, who cocreated the character.
"That is the essence of Clouseau. If you don't have that, it's hard to find a reason
for him. He never thinks he's going to fail. I really feel that's my secret."

More than once, Edwards says, he swore off Sellers. But until the actor's death
in 1980, they reunited for six films, including *The Party* (1968), a sixties bash utiliz-
ing classic conventions of comedy such as sight gags and mistaken identity. In fact,
it was originally intended as a silent film, "but the minute we got on the set and
Peter tried to do what he did," Edwards says, "it was perfectly obvious he could not
be a silent character. And I said, 'Oh, let's just do it with a script,' so we made it up
as we went along, from beginning to end. I never thought about making a silent
movie again. It was only with Peter that I considered it because we were both so
invested in silent films."

Growing up in Hollywood, the son of a studio production manager and grand-
son of a silent film director, Edwards says his unhappy childhood was ameliorated
by movies, particularly the work of the great silent clowns—Chaplin, Keaton,
Lloyd, and Laurel and Hardy.

In later years, he missed a chance to meet Laurel, and though he did come to
know Lloyd, it was not as a protégé. "We had a lot of talks but I didn't think of him
as some steppingstone to a career," the director reflects. "I wasn't at that stage.
He once told me about how they shot the famous clock scene in *Safety Last!* But I
wasn't trying to find out something that was going to benefit me, although I guess
eventually it did."

He did better when it came to Leo McCarey, who, as the director of *Duck Soup*,
Ruggles of Red Gap, and *The Awful Truth*, knew more than a little about comedy. In
fact, McCarey became something of an unofficial mentor to Edwards. He learned
from him the importance of timing, later one of the hallmarks of Edwards's
comedy.

"One day in the late 1940s or early '50s, McCarey started talking about staging
a gag," recalls Edwards. "I'd never heard anything like it. His example was a young
man and his sweetheart who had just spent a day in the park. They go to a streetcar, and he bids her off. In those days, streetcars had fixed steps, and, as she stood
on the step and said goodbye, the streetcar began moving. And he walks along with
it, all the while extolling his passion for her. But pretty soon, the streetcar picks up
too much speed, and he gets clipped from behind and lands in the middle of the
road. She keeps waving goodbye, and he's sitting disheveled in a puddle waving
back. End of joke? No. He now realizes he's in danger of getting run over, and he
does a routine of picking up the stuff that's fallen out of his pockets and putting
it into a hat. Finally, he makes it to the curb. End of joke? Not at all. Now an old
lady passing by goes through the hat, takes a pen from it and puts a nickel in the

hat. That was the end. I can't tell you how many times I've thought about that and wondered if I could top it. And if so, how?"

Edwards certainly tried in *The Great Race* (1965), his most obvious homage to the silent clowns and their antics. It's not for nothing that the dedication "For Mr. Laurel and Mr. Hardy" appears on screen even before the Warner Bros. logo. The film is replete with physical gags, but probably none more famous than the orgiastic pie fight that marks the climax of the film's *Prisoner of Zenda* subplot.

Edwards happily acknowledges his indebtedness to the silent clowns. "Absolutely," he says, "that's why it's in there—not necessarily that I was going to do it better, but that I would be original enough to do it bigger." The way Edwards planned it, everyone from Natalie Wood to Jack Lemmon to Peter Falk would quickly be covered in multicolored cream, but Tony Curtis, dressed completely in white, would remain spotless as he walked through a gauntlet of airborne desserts—until, that is, Wood lands him one square on the puss.

As it turned out, the scene worked better than Edwards had dared hoped. "It was almost magical in a way," he marvels, "because I expected to have to shoot in cuts to get Curtis to walk through this carnage and be untouched. So I did a big master shot with three cameras, and the actors threw things at him and around him, but somehow nothing ever landed on him. We got it all in one take. I think one camera was in close, one medium, and one full-shot."

Another important lesson from his silent heroes, echoed by McCarey, was the connection between pain and comedy. "When you start analyzing the great film comics," Edwards explains, "they were constantly beating each other up and falling down stairs and tripping over pants. They got their laughs through a sort of carnage, and I think I started doing that, too."

In this vein, he remembers another McCarey tale, this one a true story in which a woman with a husband in the hospital goes seeking financial assistance from a charity board on which McCarey sits. She explains how her husband's heart attack and her own arthritis have left them destitute and how her husband had become so anxious about their future that he'd asked for a cigarette, which she couldn't light for him. So he had to do it himself, right there in his oxygen tent.

"When he lit it," Edwards relates, "there was an enormous explosion that blew him right into the maternity ward. And everybody on this charity board—these dozen stern-faced people—they just broke up. McCarey said that it couldn't have been funnier. But it wasn't funny at all, of course. A man had been blown up. And from this story, I learned about pain and eliciting laughter. I paid attention, and it served me well."

Examples abound of the director incorporating these lessons in his work, with Clouseau's violent mishaps topping the list, not to mention Jack Lemmon's Prof. Fate in *The Great Race* or Dudley Moore's George Webber in *10* (1979). But with

Edwards's collaboration with Moore in 10, the story of a middle-aged man set loose in the sexual revolution, the director took the physical comedy of his earlier work and added a new level of social commentary. Still, there were plenty of pratfalls. Separating who is responsible for the laughs in a comedy is no easy task. "It's a little hard to answer who does what," says Edwards, when asked who is responsible for the laughs in a particular scene in 10 where a voyeuristic Moore gets beaned by his outdoor telescope and tumbles down a hillside, only to end up in his swimming pool once he makes it back up.

"Rolling down the hill was mine," says Edwards. "Sure, Dudley added to it, because he's Dudley. He was enormously talented. I may have written in the script something less than, or beyond, what we got to when we were shooting, but near as I can remember, that was all my stuff. But when you give a genius direction, then he brings his genius to it." By way of example, Edwards mentions the beach scene in which Moore first sees Bo Derek in a swimsuit. "When he went hopping across the hot sand, his physical reaction to a scripted moment made it that much better," the director says. "You could say Dudley elaborated on the gags. Like when he's trying to drink coffee after seeing the dentist but his mouth is frozen from the anesthetic. Though the shot was scripted, it's how he did it that made it great. I was lucky to have someone that talented to give my character life, but those moments that accentuated the life and the humor were essentially mine."

10 marked something of a turning point for Edwards as a comedy director, signaling a shift toward material that would increasingly involve male protagonists in the throes of midlife crises in films like *The Man Who Loved Women* (1983), *That's Life!* (1986), and *Skin Deep* (1989), which, despite his decision to include glow-in-the-dark condoms, he considers one of his funniest films. He gives much of the credit to the performance of John Ritter, who in one scene is nearly electrocuted by an ex-girlfriend. "You can't make anybody funny," Edwards says. "You can give them funny things to do. But they have to have the instinct to embellish and make it rich. I gave him the idea and . . . he had us all falling down laughing. It was a first take."

One film that didn't have a male hero—well not exactly—was *Victoria/Victoria* (1982), which starred Julie Andrews, Edwards's wife of almost forty years, as a down-on-her-luck cabaret singer in 1930s Paris who becomes a sensation when she starts performing as a man.

Edwards directed his wife in six films but insists it was no big deal. "I wish I could say that it was that different, but it wasn't," he maintains. "When we were working, she was a leading lady that I would go home and sleep with. We didn't have any arguments professionally that I can recall. It was always very pleasant."

Victor/Victoria was a frothy tip-of-the-hat to another of the director's idols: the incomparable Ernst Lubitsch. "Sure it was an homage to Lubitsch," Edwards says.

"You would be a fool not to acknowledge—if only to yourself—your betters. But I didn't go in saying I was going to mimic Lubitsch or be so blatant as to copy him. The film was a kind of silent acknowledgment to the genius of Lubitsch, the style and sophisticated humor and sexuality. I loved Lubitsch from the first frame I ever saw. I loved the characters. They made me feel at home."

It's a long way from the sophisticated, slightly risqué comedy of *Victor/Victoria* to today's more explicit, no-holds-barred films, but Edwards still tries to keep up at home. However, not very much of the new stuff is to his liking. "I don't feel laughter like I used to," he says. "I don't know whether it's the material or me becoming older and more grouchy. But for me, it just isn't that funny most of the time. I find it extra cruel, even beyond the man and the streetcar I described. I think we've lost sight of some of the subtle humor. Doctors acknowledge that laughter is great medicine, and for me lately there's too little of that [in movies]. But," he says, returning to where he started, "there's always Stan and Ollie."

Resources

"All Set." *Show*, May 1962.

American Film Institute. Blake Edwards Interview. Harold Lloyd Master Seminar at the AFI Seminar, May 14, 1979.

Biederman, Patricia Ward. "Director Blake Edwards Displays a Bronze Touch." *Los Angeles Times*, August 27, 1989.

Blair, Ian. "Blake Edwards' Patented Teamwork Makes *A Fine Mess* of a Comedy." *Chicago Tribune*, August 3, 1986.

"Blake Edwards and Julie Andrews: A Comprehensive Interview." *Playboy Magazine*, December 1982.

Brody, Richard. "Movie of the Week: *Experiment in Terror*." *The New Yorker*, October 7, 2015.

Cameron, Julia. "Home Movie: Blake Edwards' *Life* Is Autobiographical." *Chicago Tribune*, September 21, 1986.

Cameron, Sue. "Blake Edwards Talks about Budgets, Real and Exaggerated." *Hollywood Reporter*, 1971.

Caputo, Raffaele. "Topping the Topper: Blake Edwards." *Cinema Papers*, No. 85, November 1991.

Champlin, Charles. "Blake Edwards Is Up to His Movie Maverick Tricks Again." *Los Angeles Times*, July 26, 1988.

Chase, Chris. "Real Life Buoys *That's Life!*" *New York Times*, September 21, 1986, Section 2, pp. 1, 26.

Clarens, Carlos. "Masculine/Feminine, Feminine/Masculine." *Film Comment*, Vol. 18, No. 3 (May/June, 1982), pp. 18–19.

CNN. "*Larry King Weekend*: Interviews with Blake Edwards and Jack Valenti." Aired July 27, 2002.

D.A. "Getting Even." [Review of *S.O.B.*] *Newsweek*, July 6, 1981.

Daney, Serge. "Strange Bodies: On *The Great Race*." *Cahiers du Cinema in English*, No. 3, 1966.

Davis, J. Madison. "Peter Diamond, Peter Gunn, and Jacques Clouseau: The Crime Writing of Blake Edwards." *World Literature Today*, Vol. 85, No. 5. (September/October 2011), pp. 9–11.

Desowitz, Bill. "Blake Edwards: In the Pink." *Los Angeles Times*, November 4, 1999, pp. 16–17, 18.

Ebert, Roger. "Blake Edwards: In Memory." December 16, 2010. Retrieved from www.rogerebert.com/interviews/blake-edwards-in-memory.

Falwell, John. "The Art of Digression: Blake Edwards' *Skin Deep*." *Literature/Film Quarterly*, Vol. 24, No. 2 (1966), pp. 177–82.

Garbarino, Steve. "The Silver Panther Strikes Again." *New York Times, Fashions of the Times*, August 19, 2001, pp. 72, 74, 78, 80–81.

Gaydos, Steven. "Going Hyphenate." *The Writers Guild of America—The Hollywood Reporter*, March 18, 1988, p. S-18.

Gristwood, Sarah. "*Breakfast at Tiffany's*: 50 Years On." *The Telegraph*. September 30, 2010. Retrieved from www.telegraph.co.uk/culture/film/classic-movies/8032801/Breakfast-at -Tiffany-50-years-on.html

Gristwood, Sarah, and Hubert de Givenchy. "*Breakfast at Tiffany's*": The Official 50th Anniversary *Companion*. New York: Rizzoli, 2011.

Haddad-Garcia, George. "Blake Edwards Super Director." *Hollywood Studio Magazine*, November 1982, pp. 16–17.

Harmetz, Aljean. "Blake Edwards, Prolific Comedy Direction, Dies at 88." *The New York Times*, December 16, 2010.

———. "Writer of *10* Criticizes Studio's Ads." *New York Times*, October 18, 1979, p. C15.

Hauduroy, Jean-François. "Sophisticated Naturalism—Interview with Blake Edwards." *Cahiers du Cinema in English*, No. 3, 1966, pp. 20–26. (originally *Cahiers du Cinema*, #175, February 1966).

"Hollywood Intrigue . . . and the *Loser* Gets $3½ M." *New York Post*, April 16, 1984.

Honeycutt, Kirk. "His Pain, His Gain." *Los Angeles Times Calendar Section*, May 5, 1991, pp. 5, 23–27.

Horne, Jed. "Portrait: Blake Edwards." *Life*, August 1983.

Hyams, Joe. "The Edwardian Look." *New York Herald Tribune*, November 29, 1959, pp. 60–62.

"Julie Andrews and Blake Edwards: A Private Conversation." *The Hollywood Reporter 49th Annual*, pp. 98, 100.

Kehr, Dave. "Faulty *Switch*: Blake Edwards' Latest Seems Burned Out." *Chicago Tribune*, May 10, 1991.

Kennedy, Harlan. "Blake Edwards: Life After *10*." *American Film* (July–August 1981), pp. 24–28.

King, Susan. "An Active Imagination: Writer, Director, and Producer Blake Edwards, 81, and Busy, Will Receive a Lifetime Achievement Oscar." *Los Angeles Times*, December 25, 2003.

Lamb, Gregory M. "Short Takes: Inspector Clouseau Dons Dancing Shoes." *The Christian Science Monitor*, June 23, 2000.

Le Blanc, Rena. "*S.O.B.*: Blake Edwards' Blast at His Real-Life Blacklisting." *Los Angeles*, Vol. 24, No. 5, May 1979, pp. 292–93.

Lehman, Peter and William Luhr. "J'écris sur ce que je sais": Entretien avec Blake Edwards. *Positif*, Vol. 347, janvier 1990, pp. 26-36.

Lehman, Peter, and William Luhr. *Blake Edwards* (vol. 1). Athens, OH: Ohio University Press, 1981.

———. *Blake Edwards: Returning to the Scene* (vol. 2). Athens, OH: Ohio University Press, 1989.

Liebenson, Donald. "*10*—Count 'Em: Blake Edwards Films at Cannes Festival Available on Home Video." *Chicago Tribune*, May 12, 1992.

Maslin, Janet. "It's Not Just a Man's World for Blake Edwards." *New York Times (Sunday)*, May 5, 1991, Section 2, p. 24.

Meeley, Darrah. "Director—Writer—Producer—Husband—Father & Former Actor: Blake Edwards." *Screen Actor* (Spring 1987), p. 17.

Meisel, Myron. "8 by Blake Edwards." Notes for a Blake Edwards Retrospective at the Museum of Modern Art Department of Film, March 5–15, 1981.

———. "Blake Edwards." In Jean Pierre Coursodon and Pierre Sauvage, *American Directors*. New York: McGraw-Hill Companies, 1983.

———. "*S.O.B.*: Do They Mean the Movie or Blake Edwards?" *Rolling Stone*, August 6, 1981.

Mermelstein, David. "Blake Edwards Looks Back." *The Wall Street Journal*, March 5, 2009.

———. "Old School." Blake Edwards Profile. Directors Guild of America. Summer 2009.

Miller, John M. TCM Film Article: *Experiment in Terror*. www.tcm.com.

Moore, Dudley, and Dan Yakir. "Dudley Moore Gets Serious: Dudley Moore Interviewed by Dan Yakir." *Film Comment*, Vol. 15, No. 6 (November/December, 1979), pp. 52–55.

Morgan, Kim. "Sad Men: Jack Lemmon and *Days of Wine and Roses*." The Blog, February 6, 2013. www.huffpost.com.

Ng, David. "'The Art of Blake Edwards' at the Pacific Design Center." *Los Angeles Times*, January 18, 2009.

Parsons, Louella, and Harriet Parsons. "Blake Edwards: Busted Budgets Are Box Office." *New York Journal-American Pictorial Living*, June 20, 1965.

"Proust Questionnaire: Blake Edwards." *Vanity Fair*, March 2004.

Rickey, Carrie. "Let Yourself Go! Three Musicals Sing One From the Libido." *Film Comment*, Vol. 18, No. 2 (March–April, 1982), pp. 43–47.

Roberts, Jerry. "The Clouseau Gene" (Blake Edwards Tribute). *The Hollywood Reporter*, October 22, 1993, pp. T-14, T-16.

Roberts, Jerry. "Pure Blake" (Blake Edwards Tribute). *The Hollywood Reporter,* October 22, 1993, pp. T-1–3, T-8.

Rosenfield, Paul. "Reconcilable Differences." *Los Angeles Times Calendar Section*, July 12, 1987.

Sanello, Frank. "In *That's Life!* Jennifer Edwards Relives Her Battles with the Film Director Dad Who Once Rejected Her." *People*, Vol. 26, No. 15, October 13, 1986. Retrieved from www .people.com.

Sarris, Andrew. "Blake Edwards." *The American Cinema: Directors and Directions, 1929–1968*. New York: Dutton, 1968.

———. "The Bitter Essence of Blake Edwards." *Village Voice*, May 5, 1987, pp. 59, 99.

Schweiger, Daniel. "Jimmy Smits and Blake Edwards—*Switch*'s Real Men." *Entertainment Today*, April 12, 1991.

Smith, Sid. "Double Play: Julie Andrews, Blake Edwards Lead the Team Taking Musical *Victor/Victoria* to Broadway." *Chicago Tribune*, July 16, 1995.

Stamelman, Peter. "Blake Edwards Interview—In the Lair of the Pink Panther." *Millimeter*, January 1977, pp. 18–20, 22, 72–75.

Stirling, Richard. *Julie Andrews: An Intimate Biography*. New York: St. Martin's Griffin, 2009.

Thomson, David. "The Rest Is Sellers." *Film Comment*, Vol. 16, No. 5 (September–October 1980), pp. 30–32.

Ulmer, James. "Edwards the Outcast Finds Haven in Cannes." *The Hollywood Reporter*, May 14, 1992.

Wasson, Sam. *A Splurch in the Kisser: The Movies of Blake Edwards*. Middletown, CT: Wesleyan
University, 2009.

Weiler, A. H. "The Screen: *Breakfast at Tiffany's*: Audrey Hepburn Stars in Music Hall Comedy."
The New York Times, October 6, 1961.

Werrett, June. "Great Directors: Blake Edwards." *Senses of Cinema*, Issue 24 (January 2003).
Retrieved from senses of cinema.com/2003/great-directors/Edwards/.

Wilmington, Michael. "*That's Life!* A Family Affair." *Los Angeles Times*, September 26, 1986.
Retrieved from www.latimes.com1986-09-26/entertainment/ca-1936_1_movie-review.

Wunrow, Zachary B. "Holly Golightly and the Endless Pursuit of Self-Actualization in *Breakfast at
Tiffany's*." *Inquiries*, Vol. 6, No. 9, 2014, pp. 1–3. Retrieved from www.inquiriesjournal.com.

Young, Jordan. "Inspector Clouseau Strikes Again—and Again and Again." *New York Times*, July
16, 1978, pp. D-15, D-24.

Index

CPSIA information can be obtained
at www.ICGtesting.com
Printed in the USA
BVHW030844211219
567152BV00001B/3/P

9 781496 825605